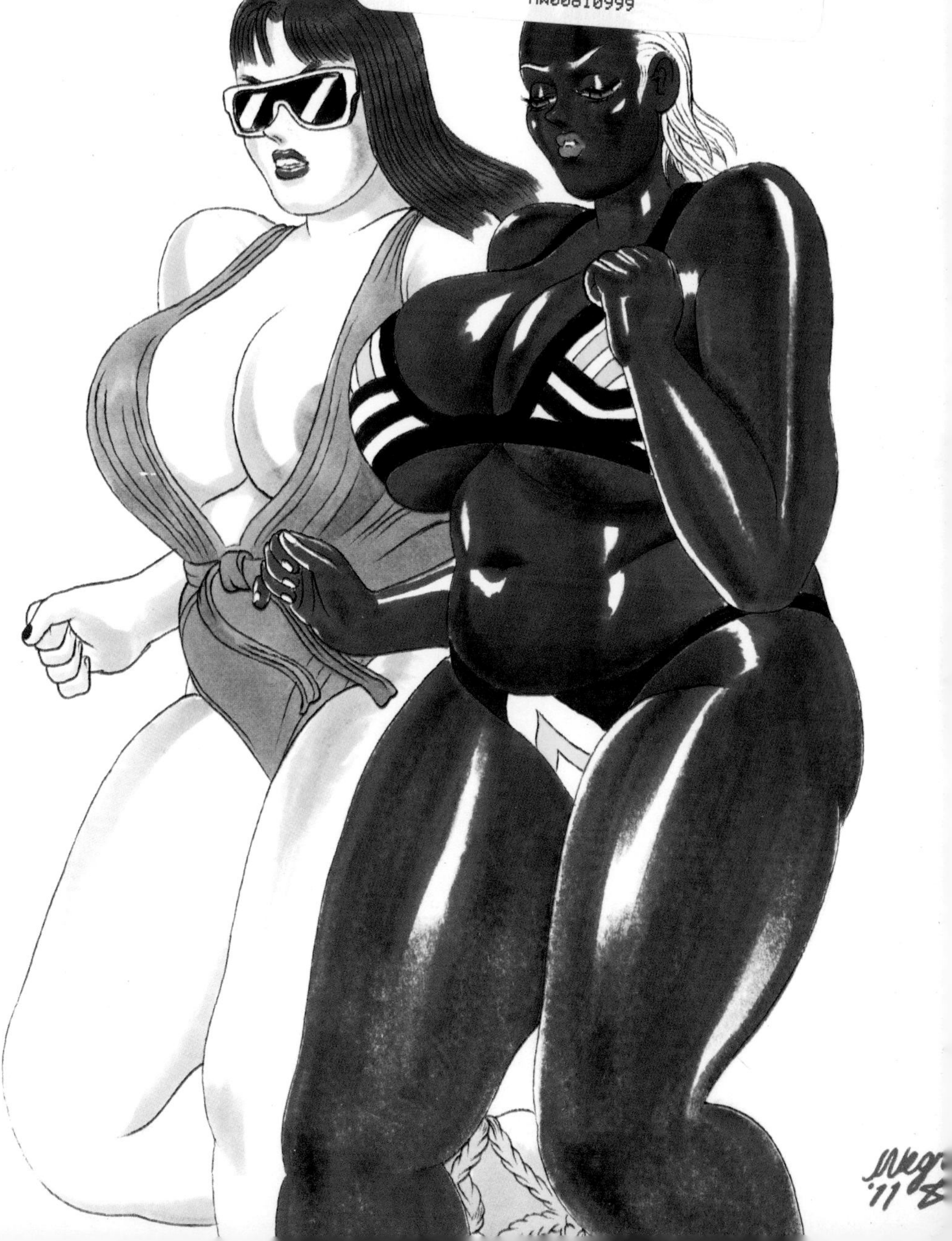

jonnynegron.tumblr.com
pictureboxinc.com
normanhathaway.com

First Edition October 2012.

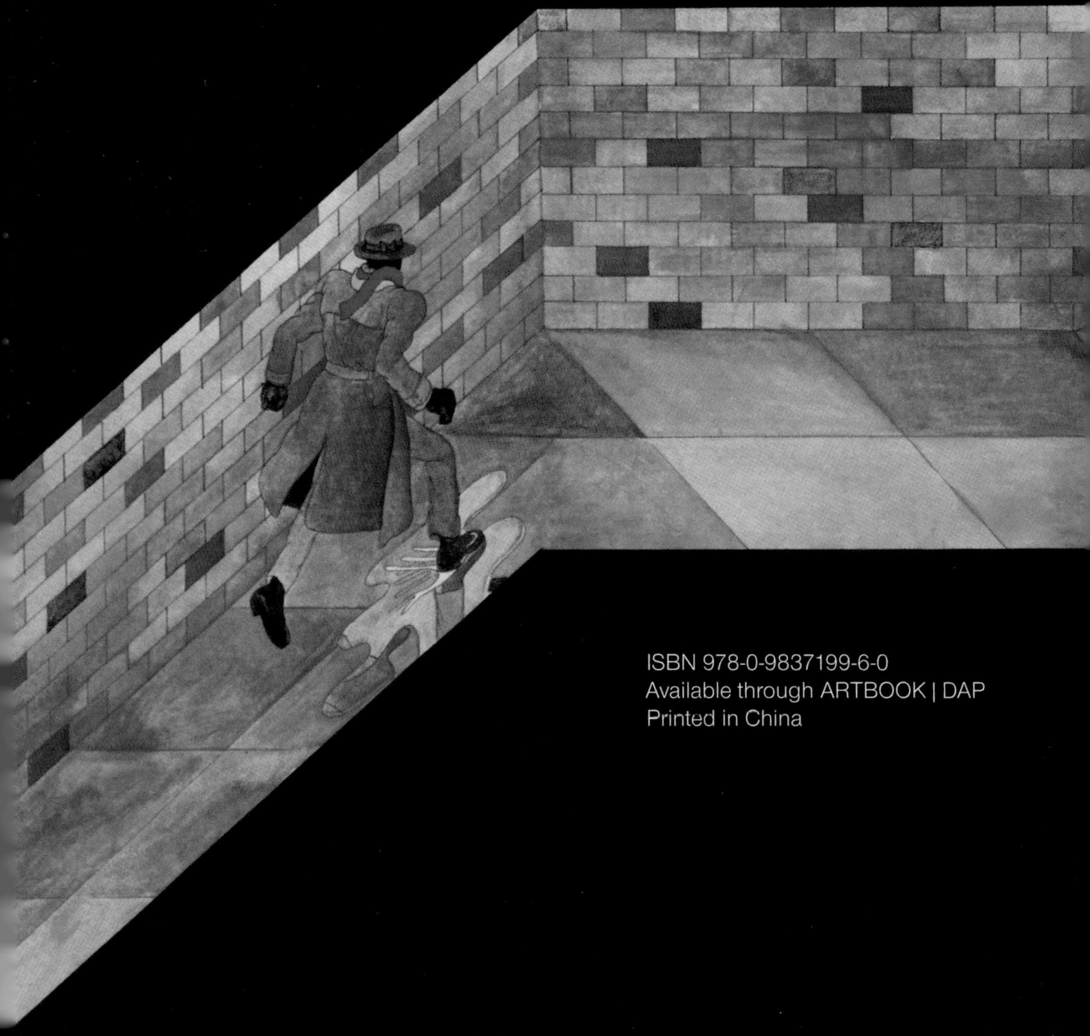

ISBN 978-0-9837199-6-0
Available through ARTBOOK | DAP
Printed in China

Editor: Dan Nadel
Creative Director: Norman Hathaway

PictureBox
PO Box 24744
Brooklyn, New York 11202

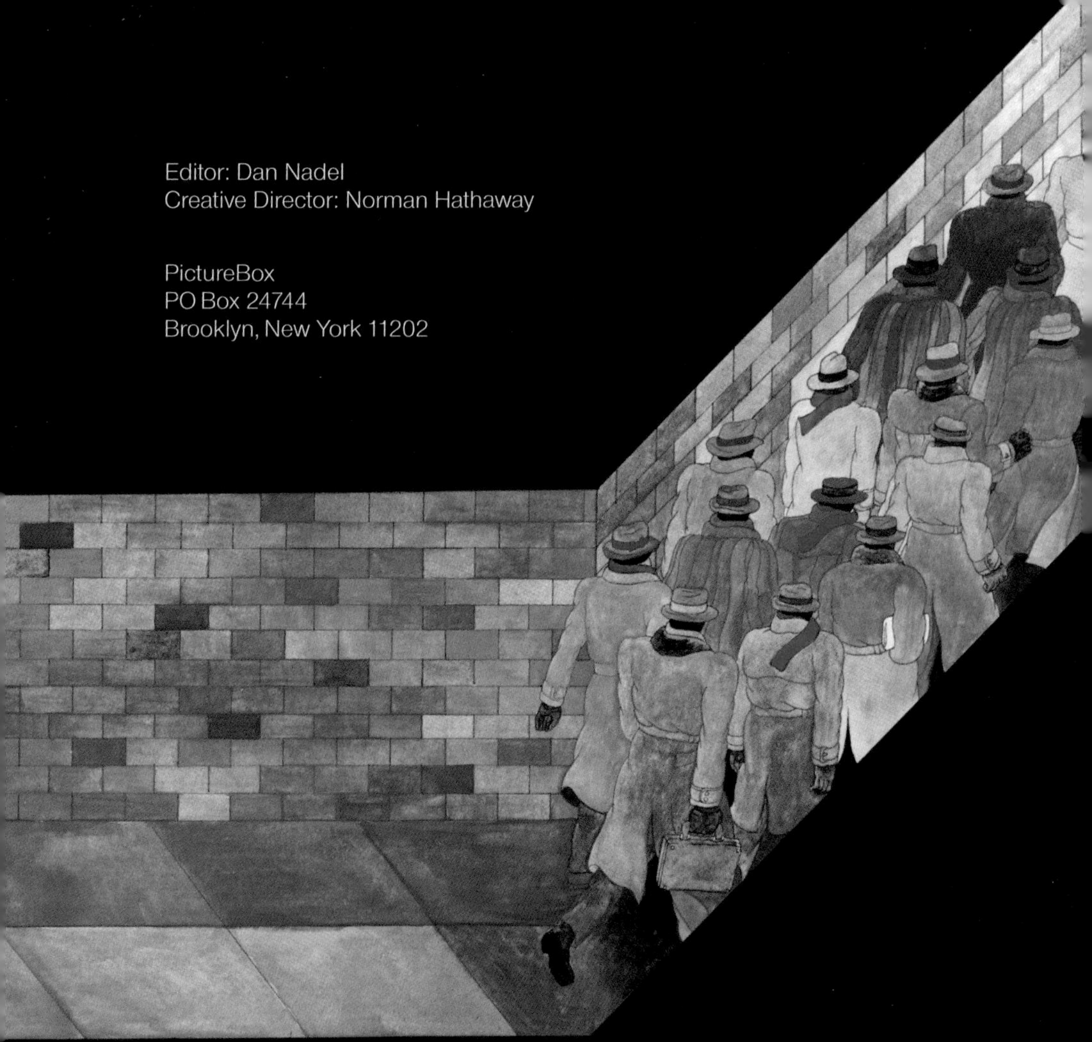

NEGRON

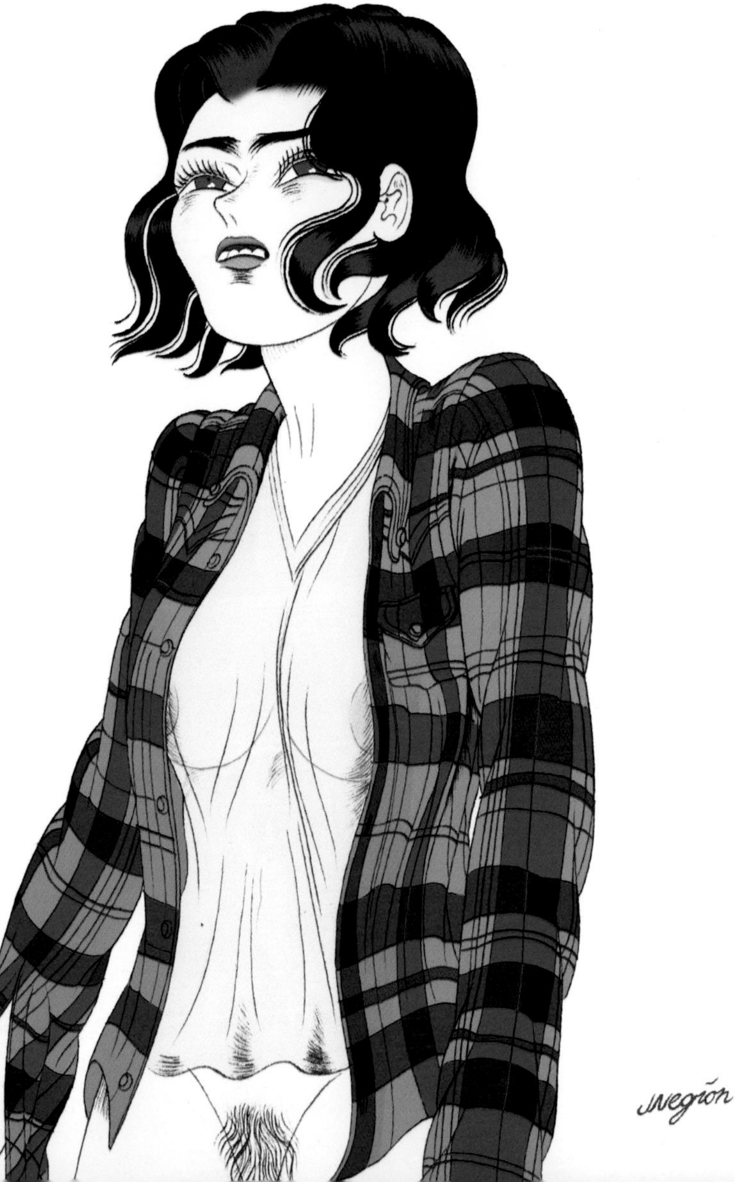

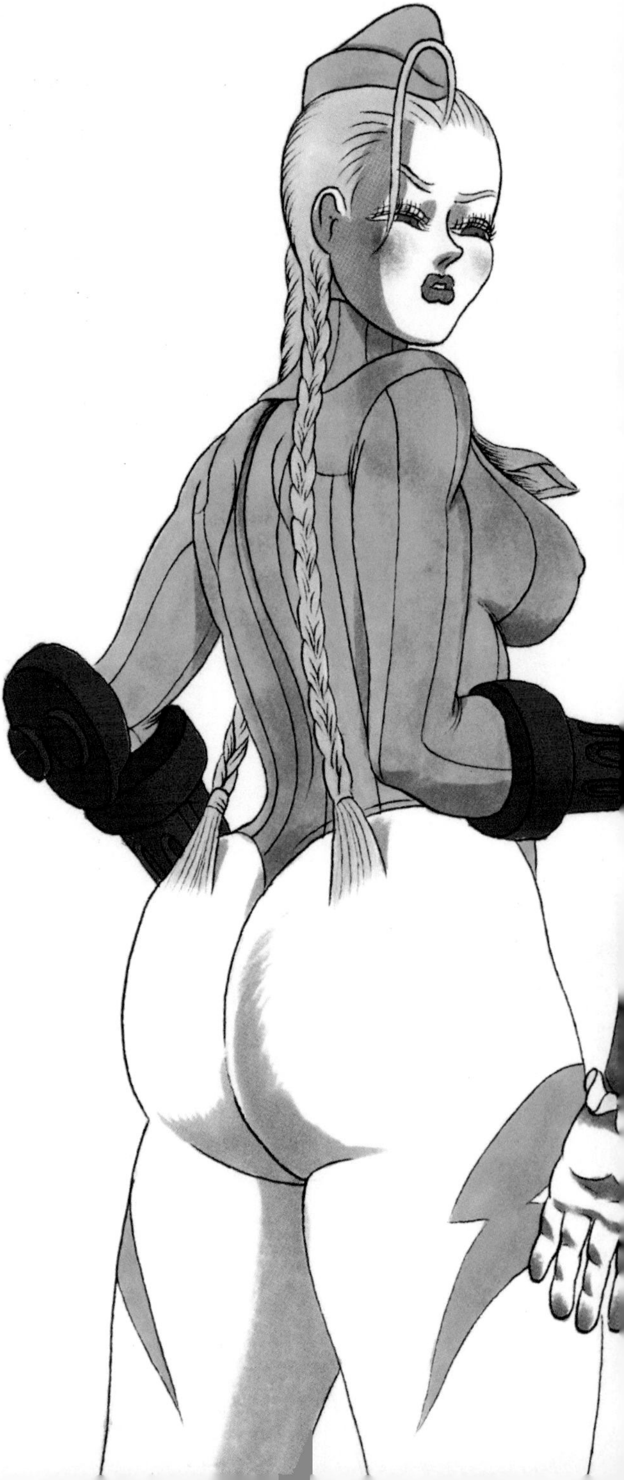

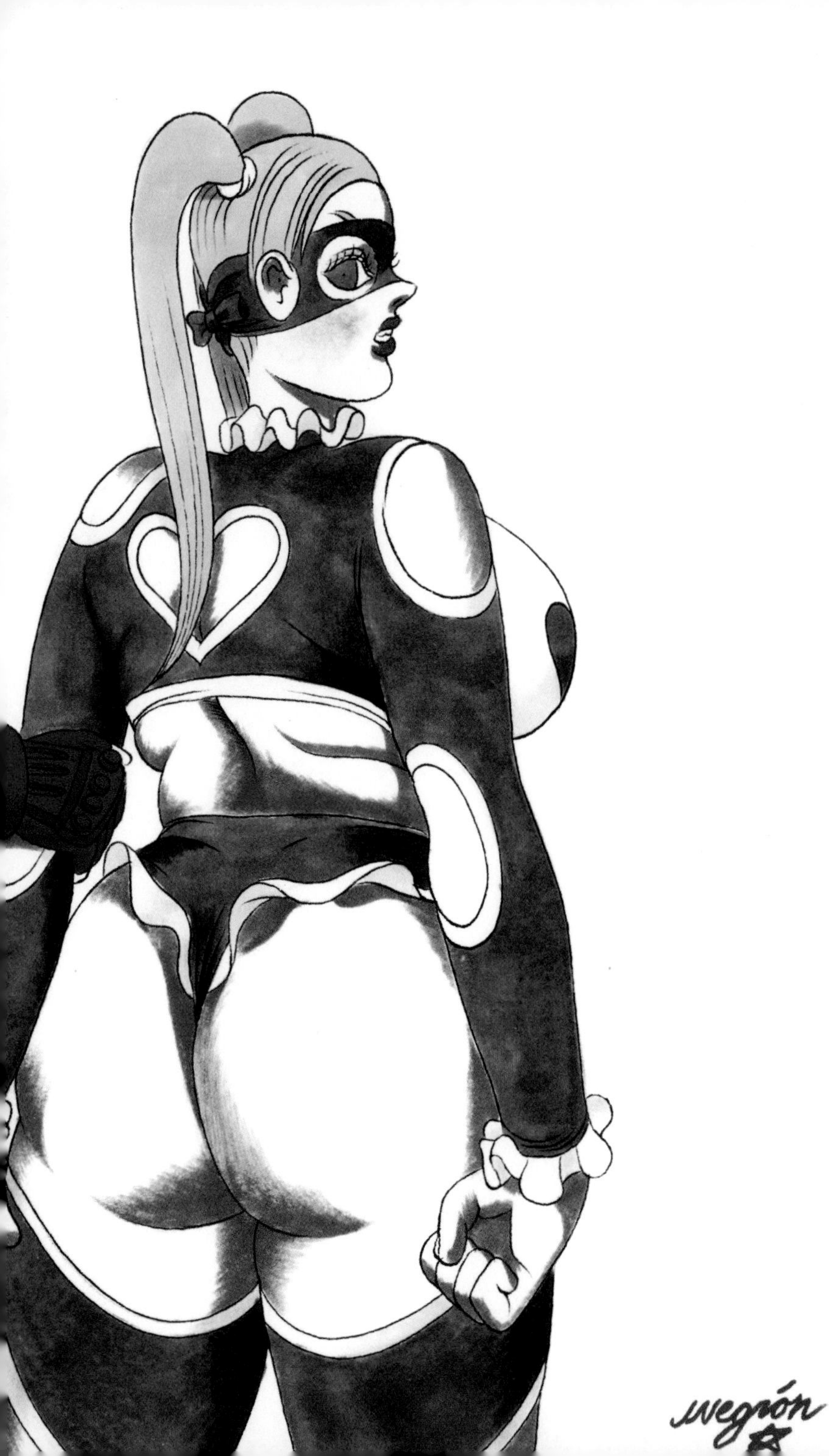
wegrón

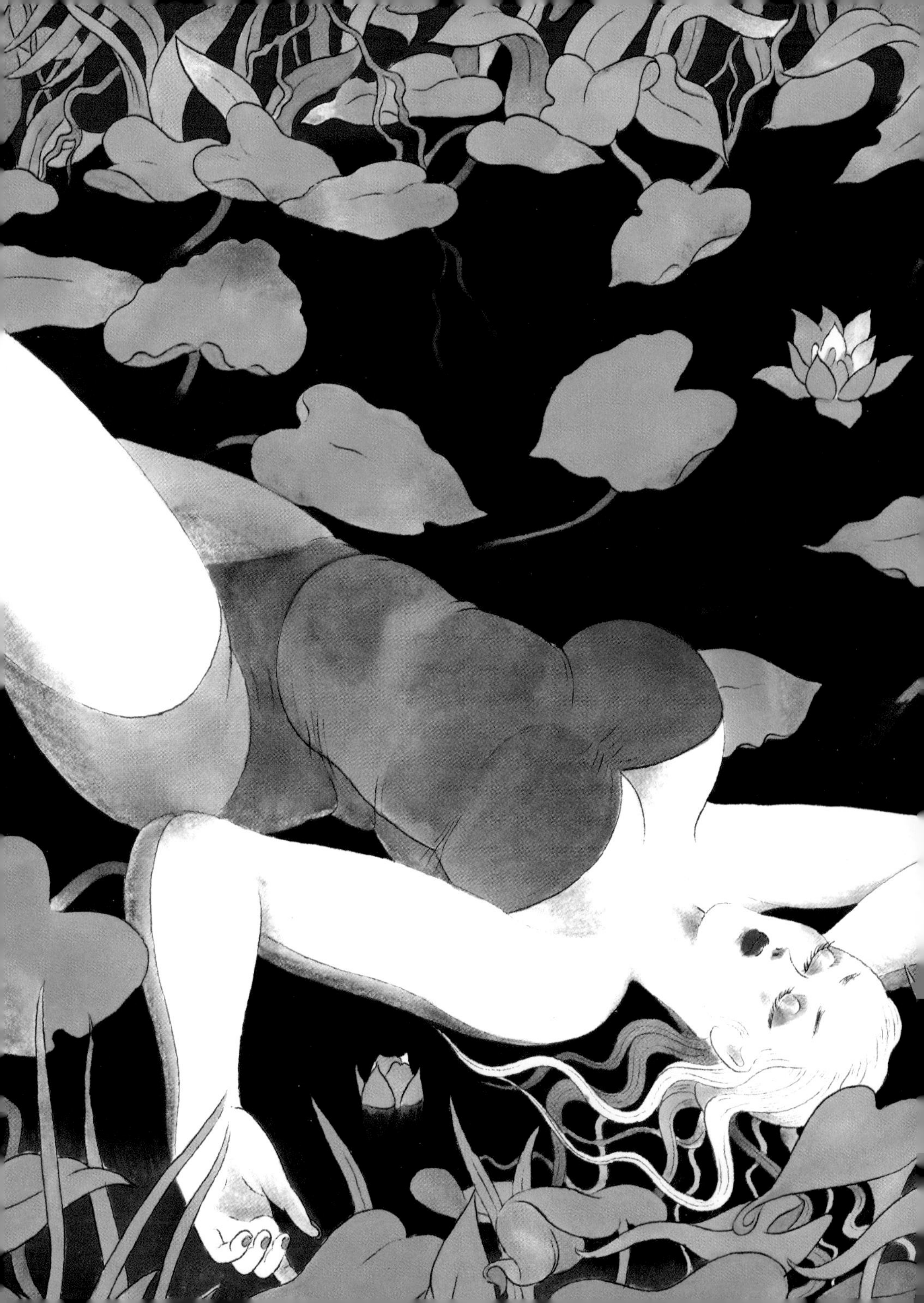

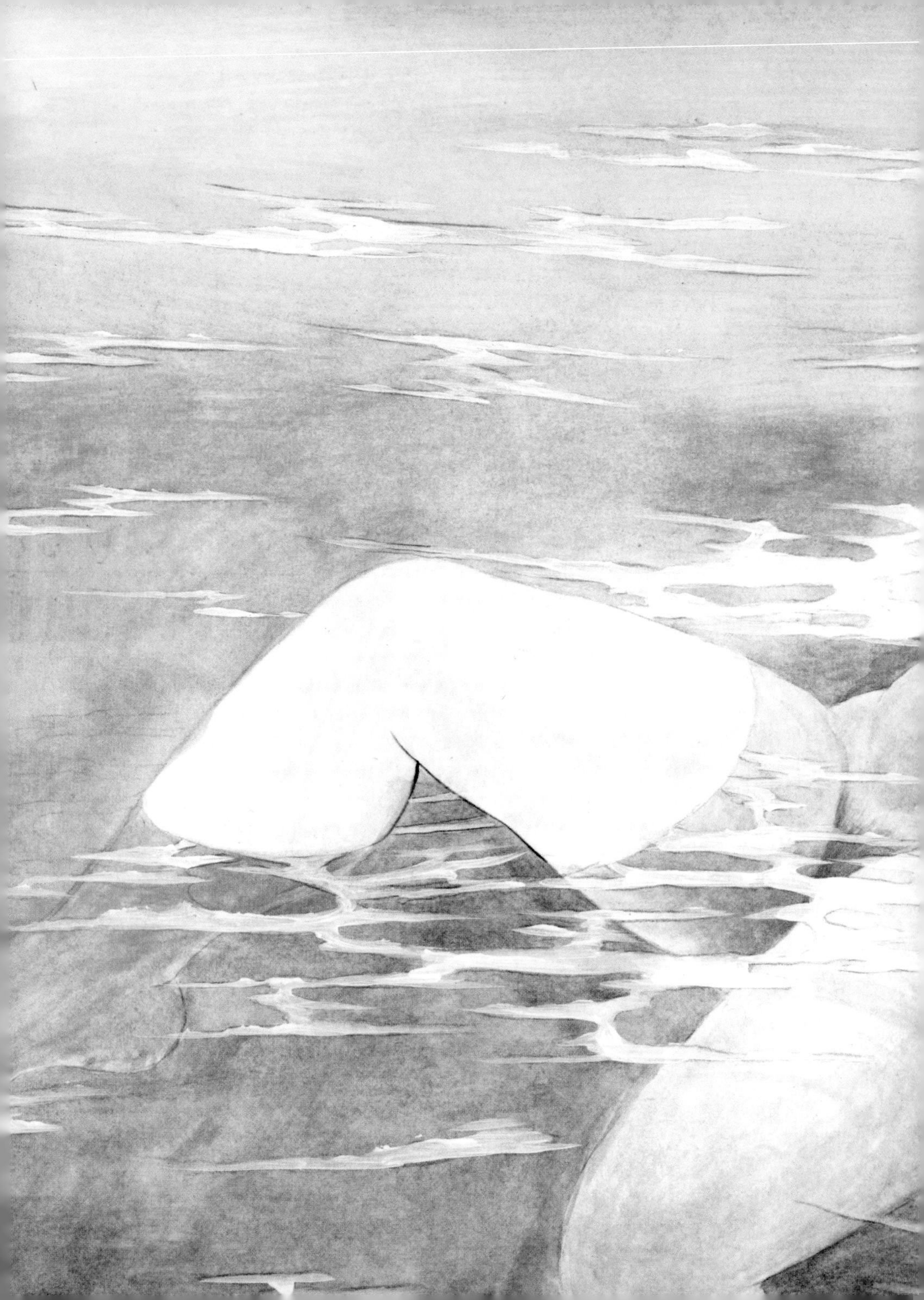

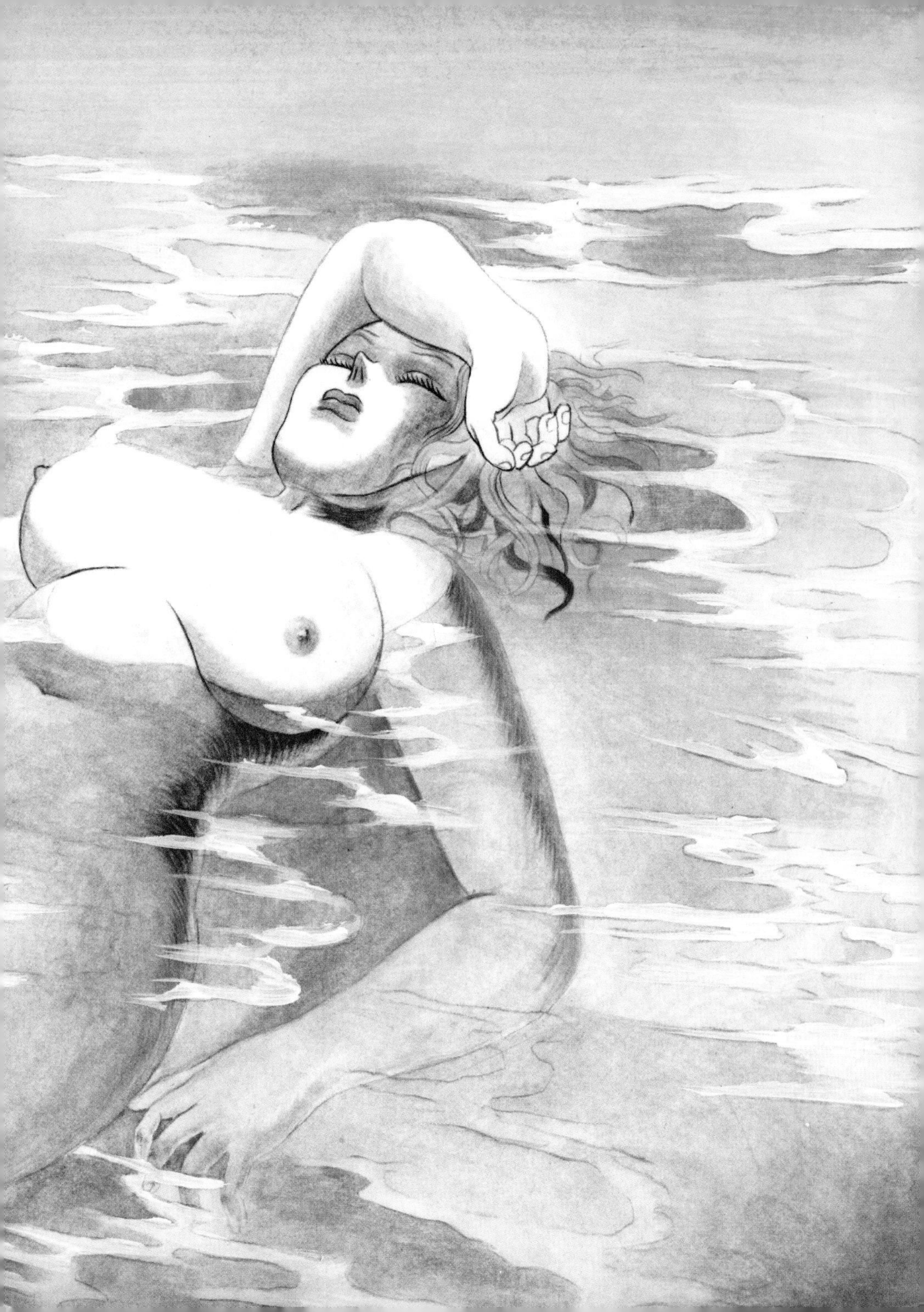

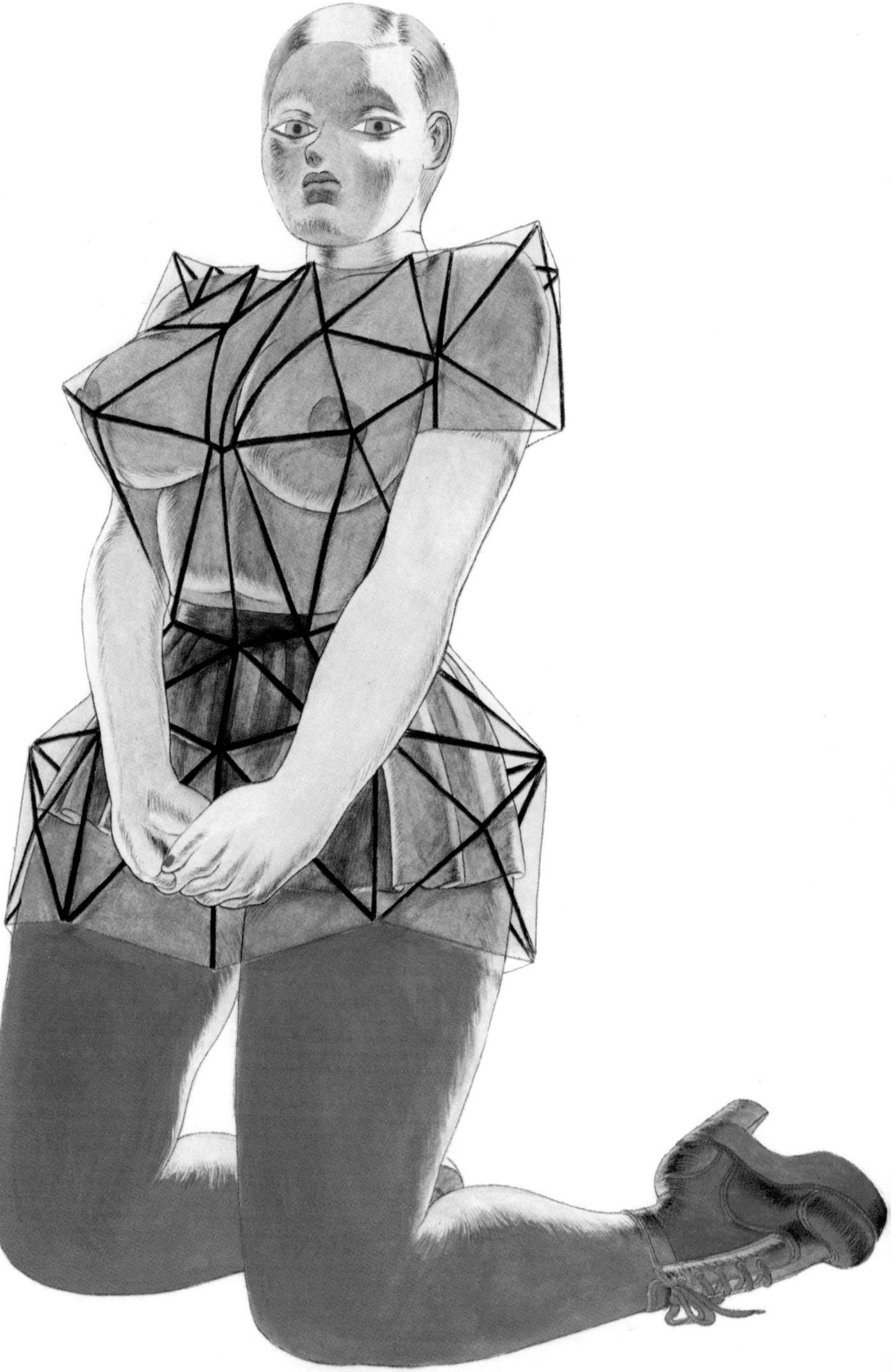

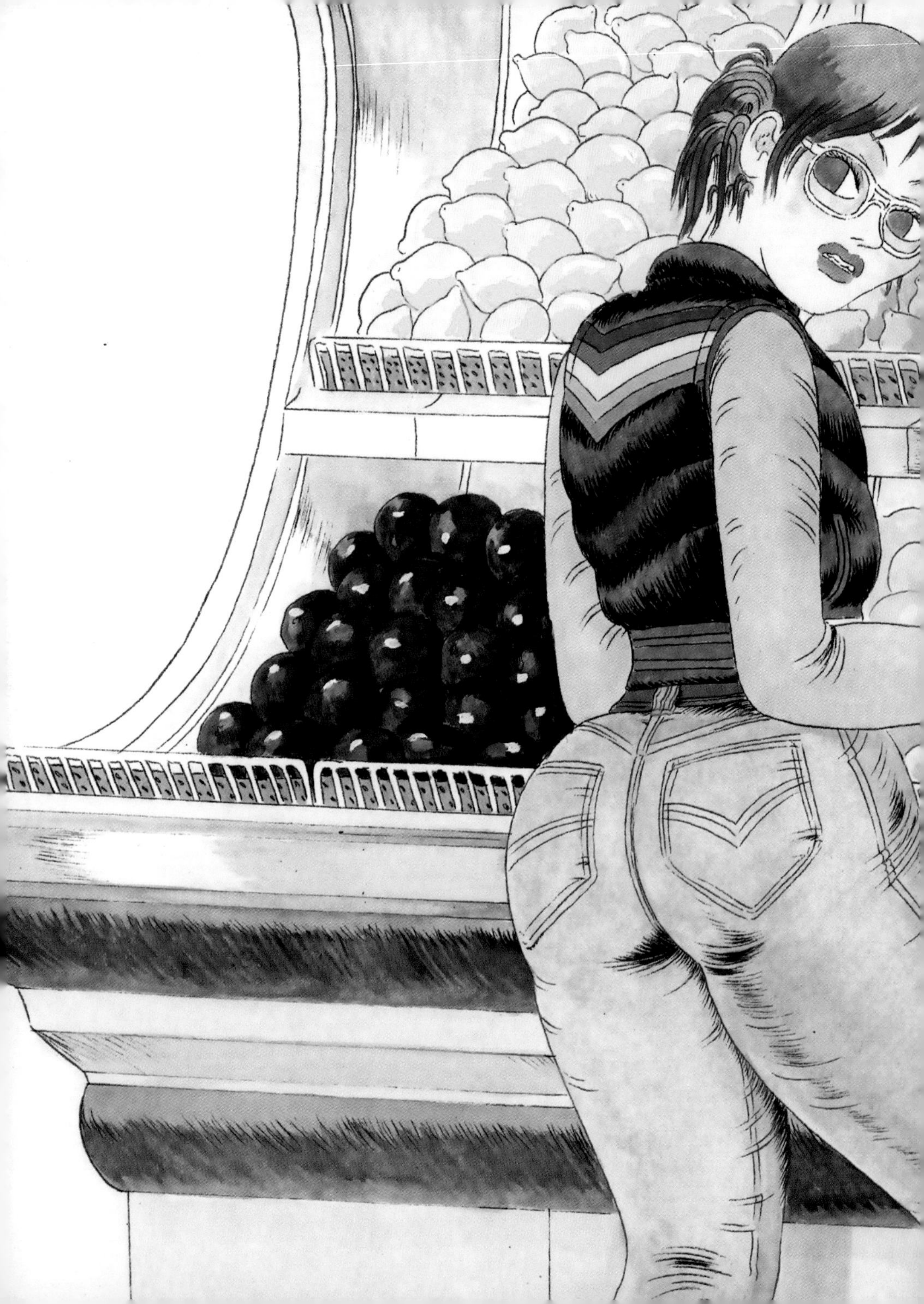

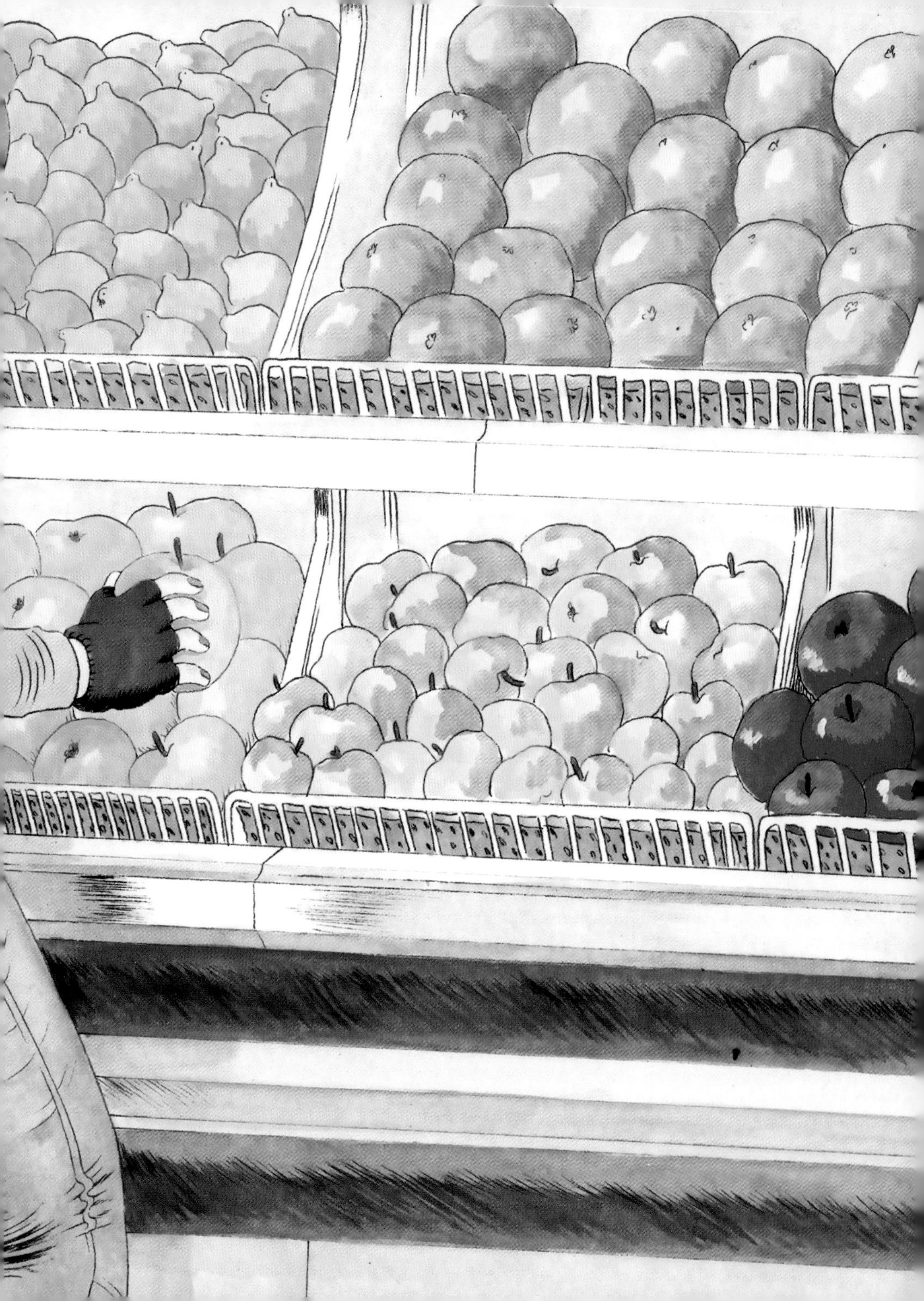

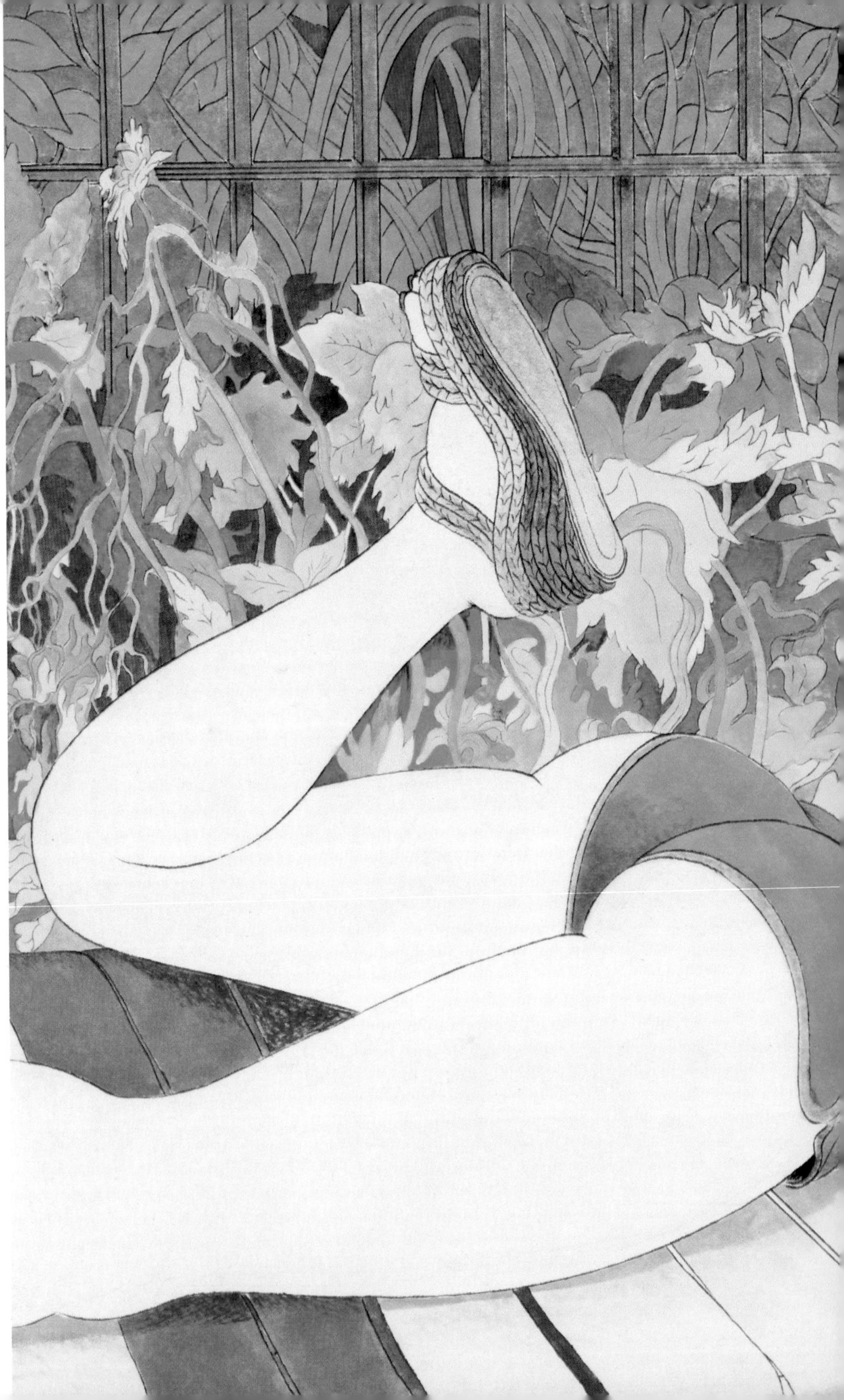

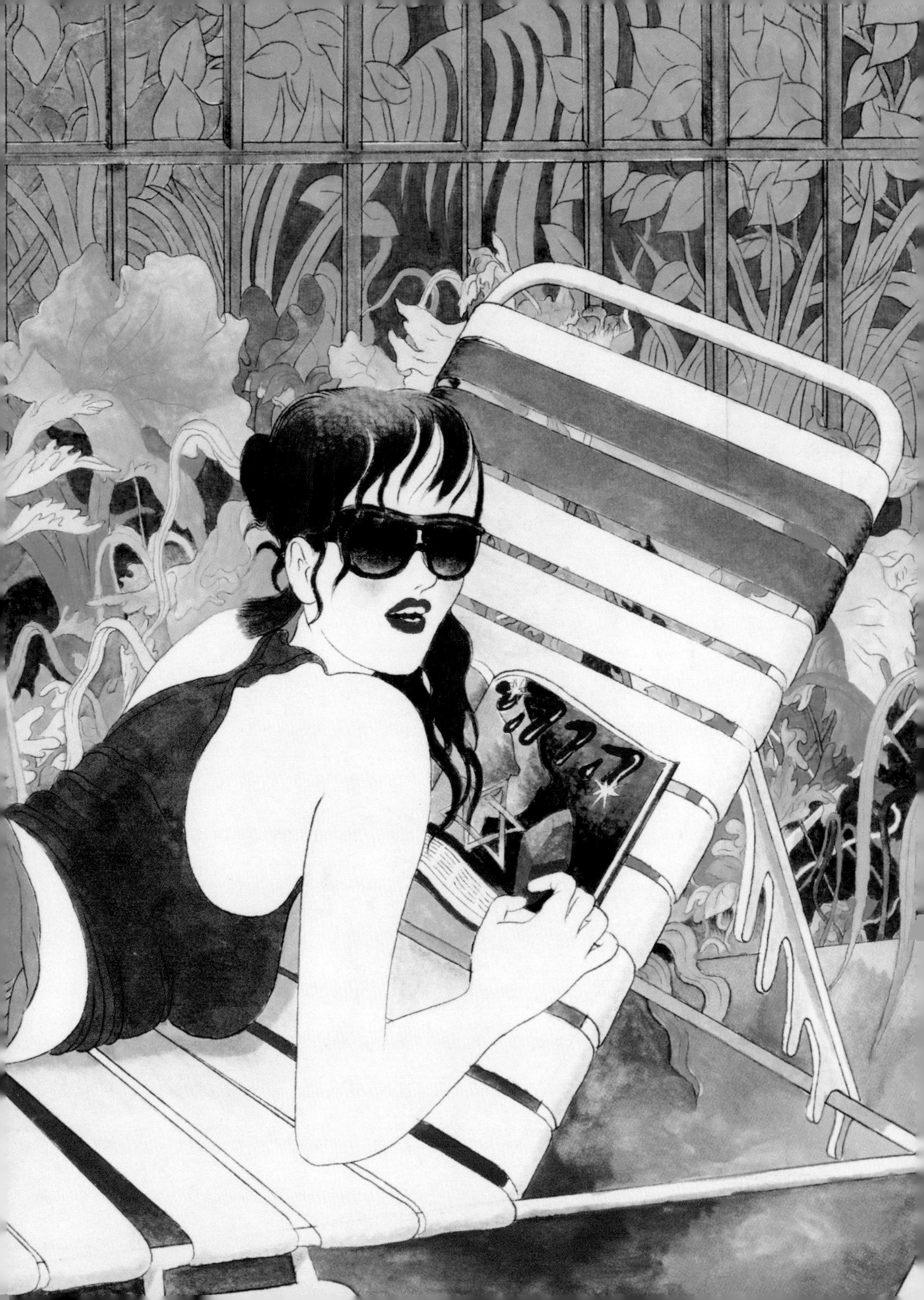

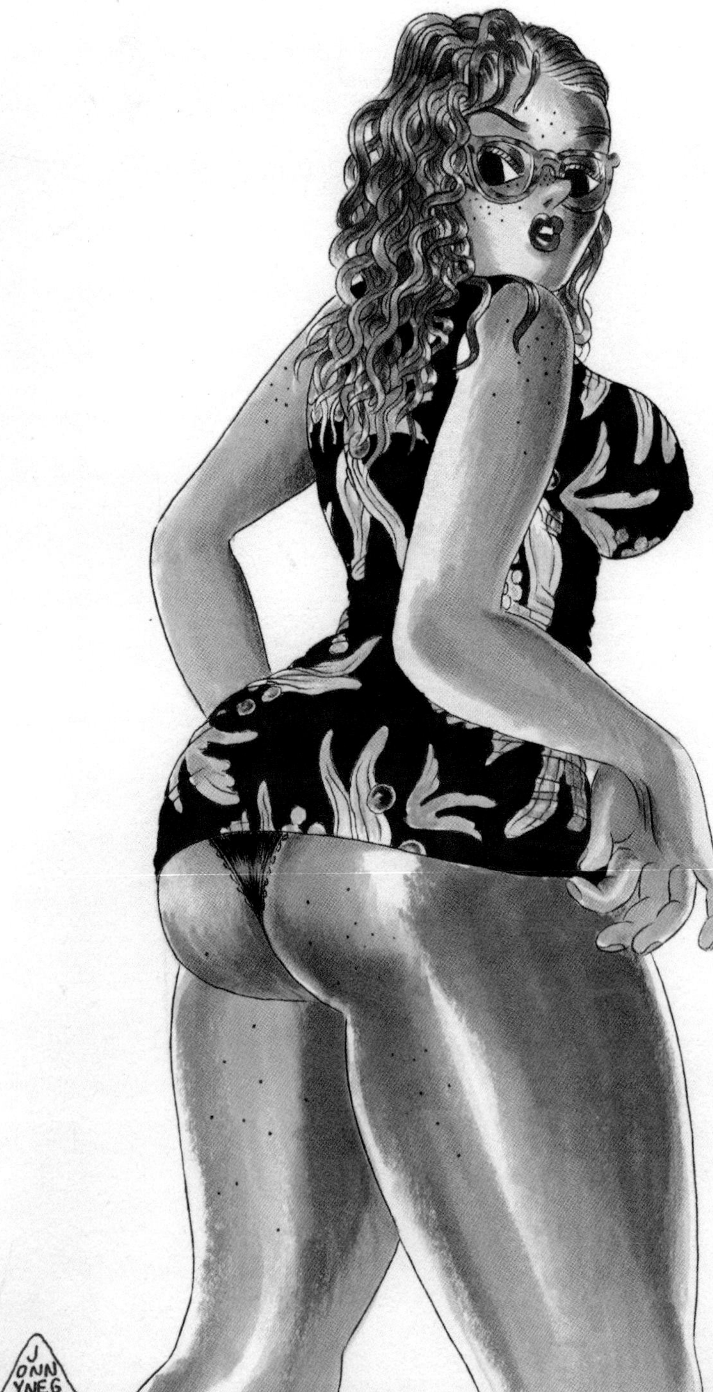
J
ONN
YNEG
RON '11

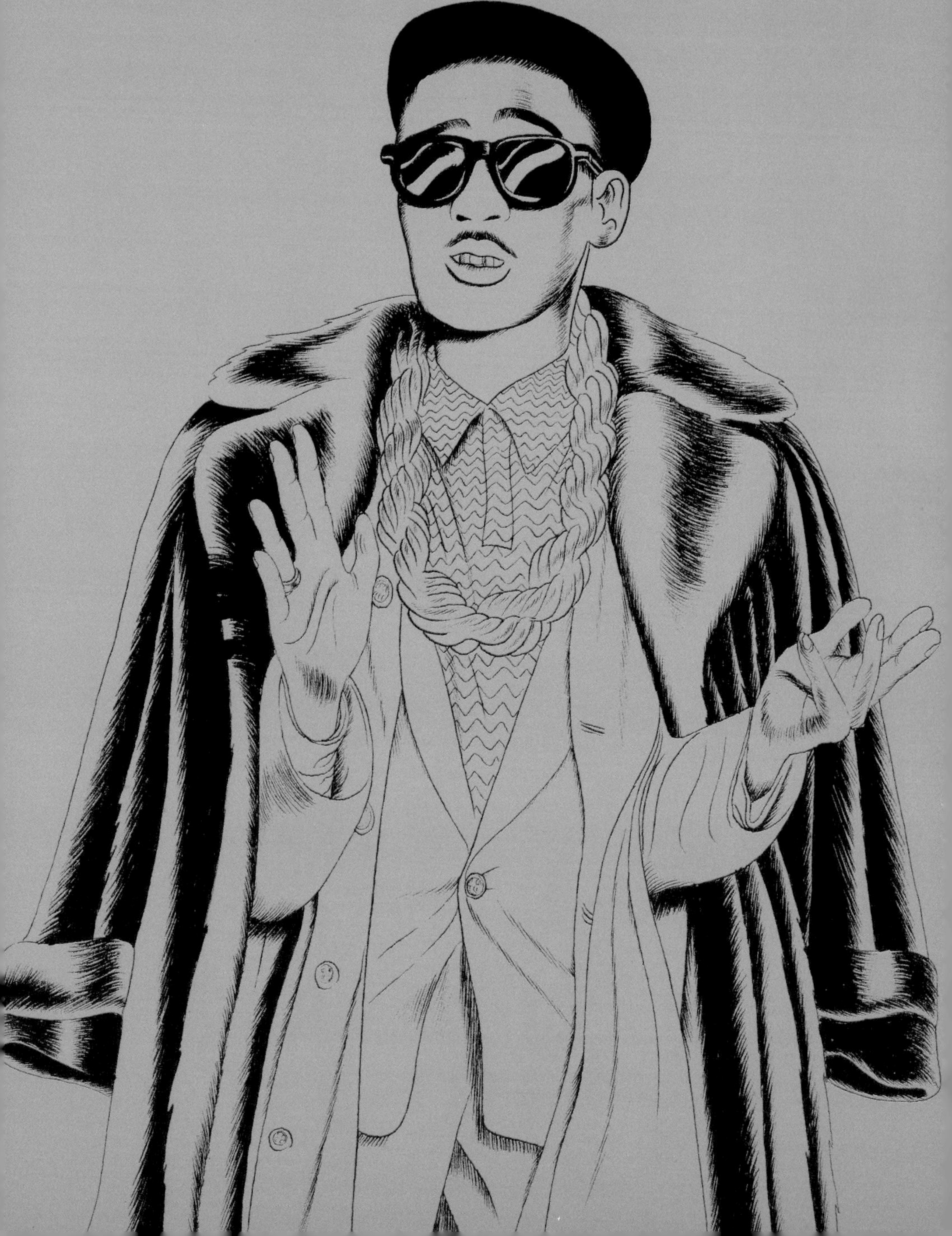

VIOLENCE

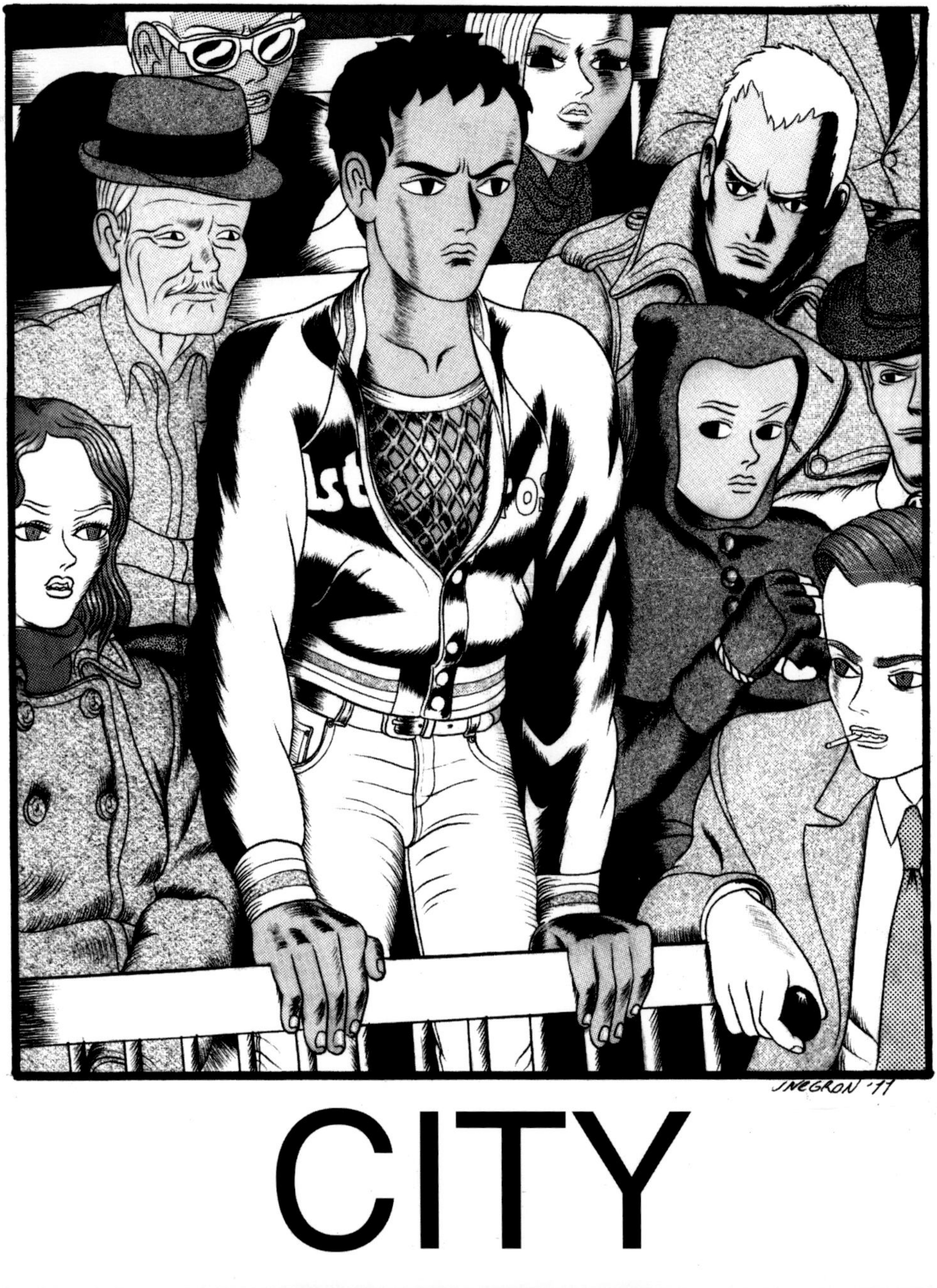
JNEGRON '11

CITY

HEY... WAKE UP... YOU'RE COVERED IN SWEAT...

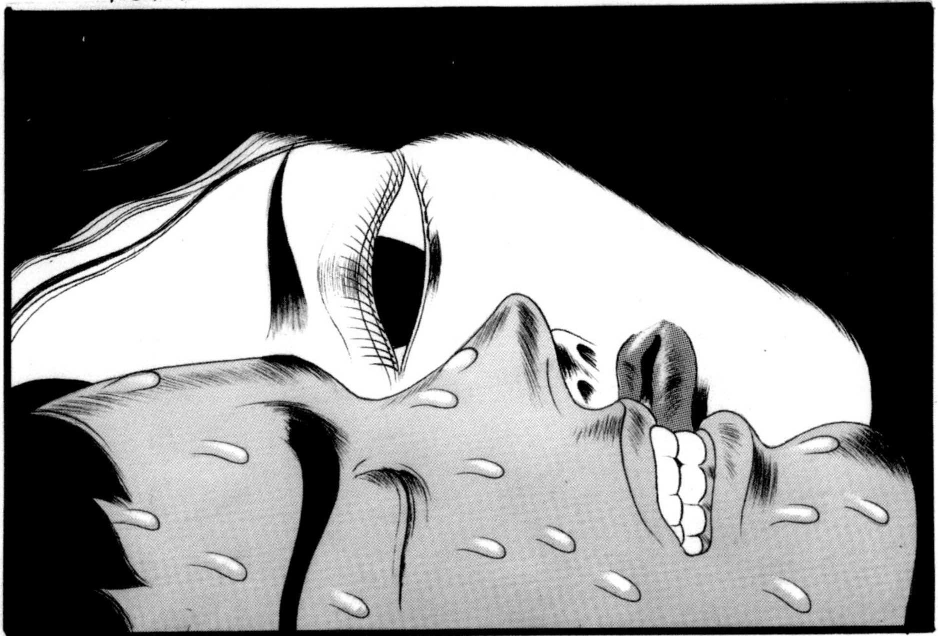

...I WAS HAVING A TERRIBLE DREAM...

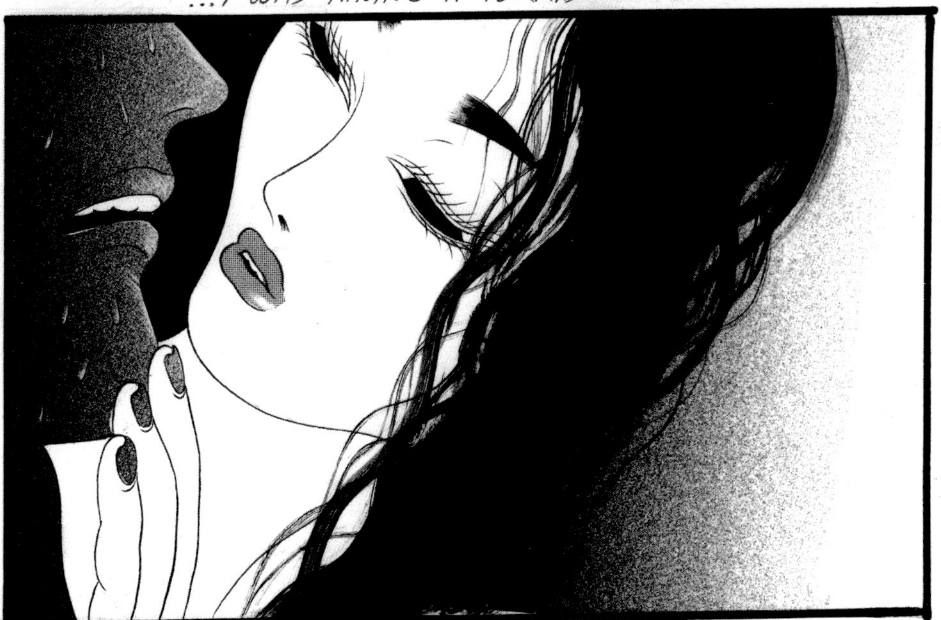

TELL ME ABOUT IT...

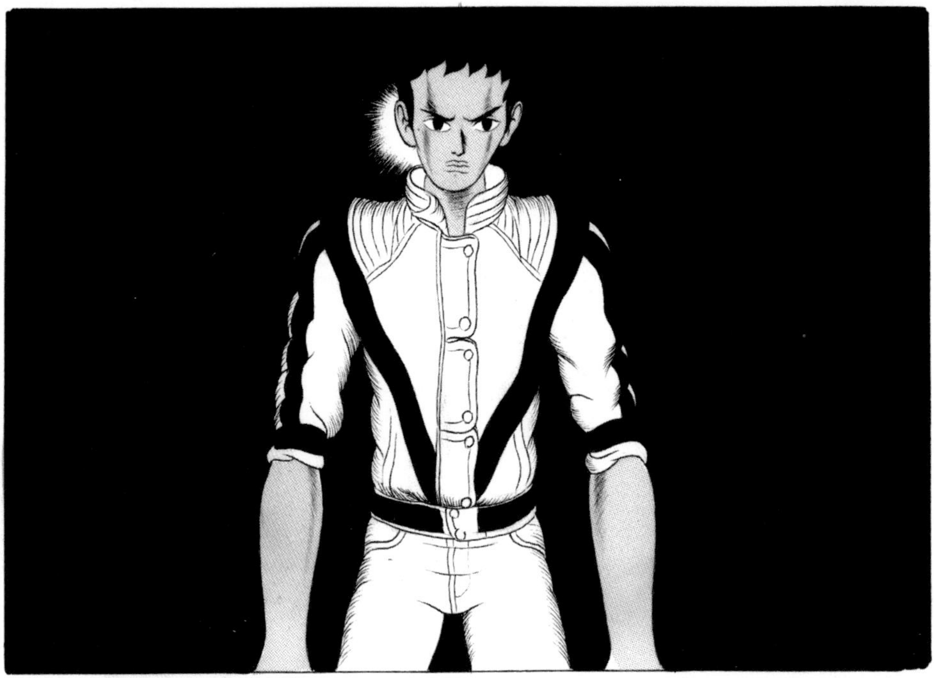

I'M WALKING DOWN THIS STREET, WEARING THE SAME OUTFIT
MICHAEL JACKSON WORE IN THE THRILLER VIDEO...

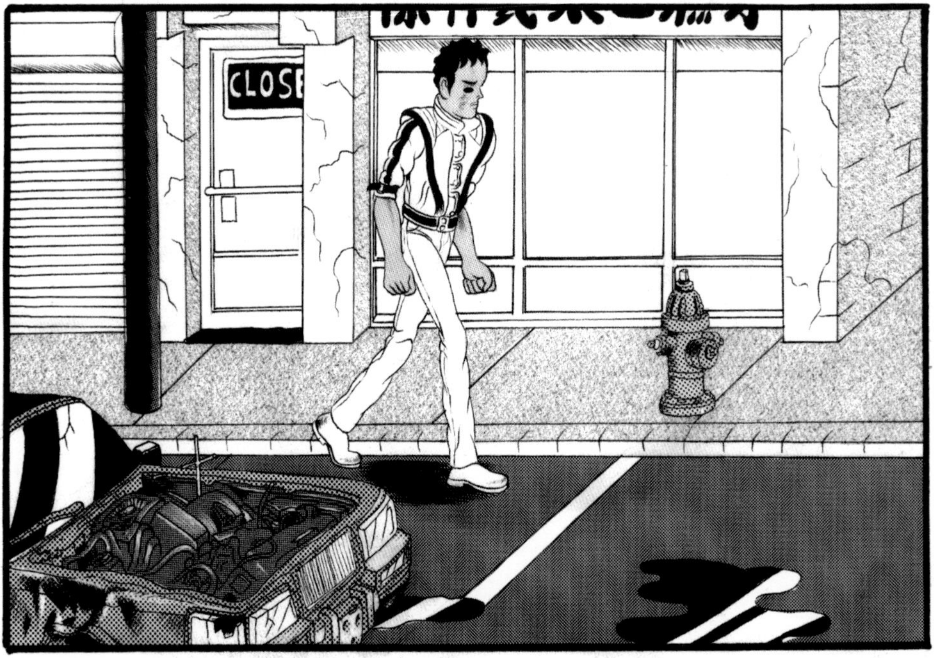
CLOSE

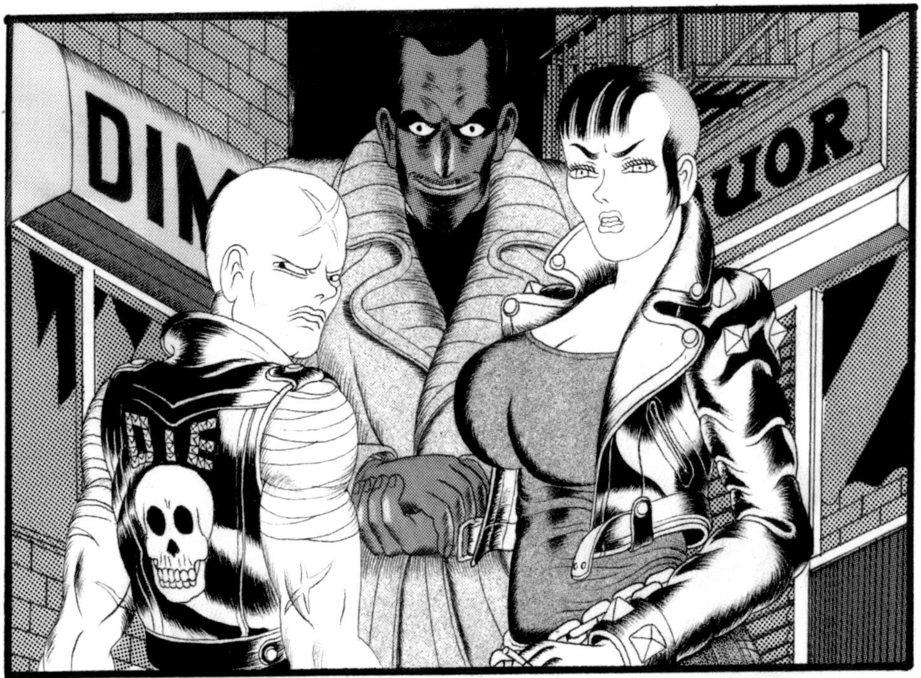
DIM
UOR
DIE

THEN, I COME ACROSS SOME PEOPLE HANGING OUT IN THE MIDDLE OF THE STREET... THEY LOOK **MALICIOUS...**

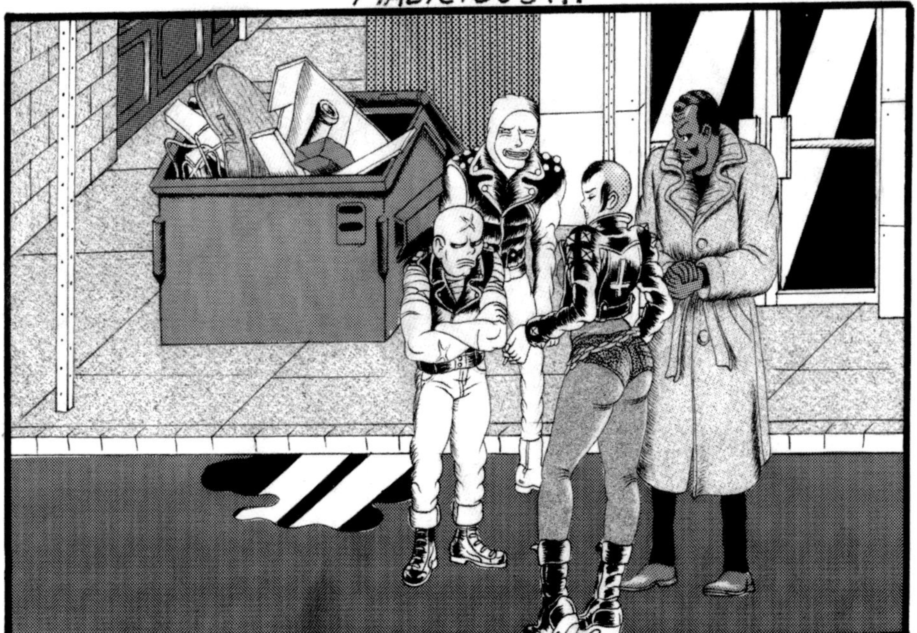

AS I GET CLOSER, I'M SURROUNDED BY THE THUGS...

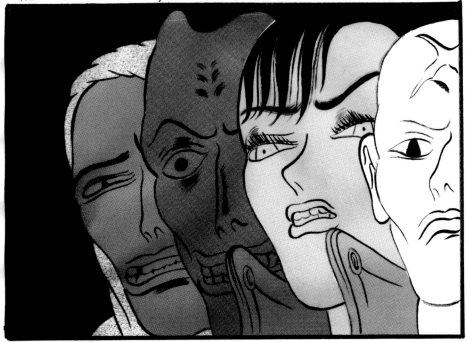

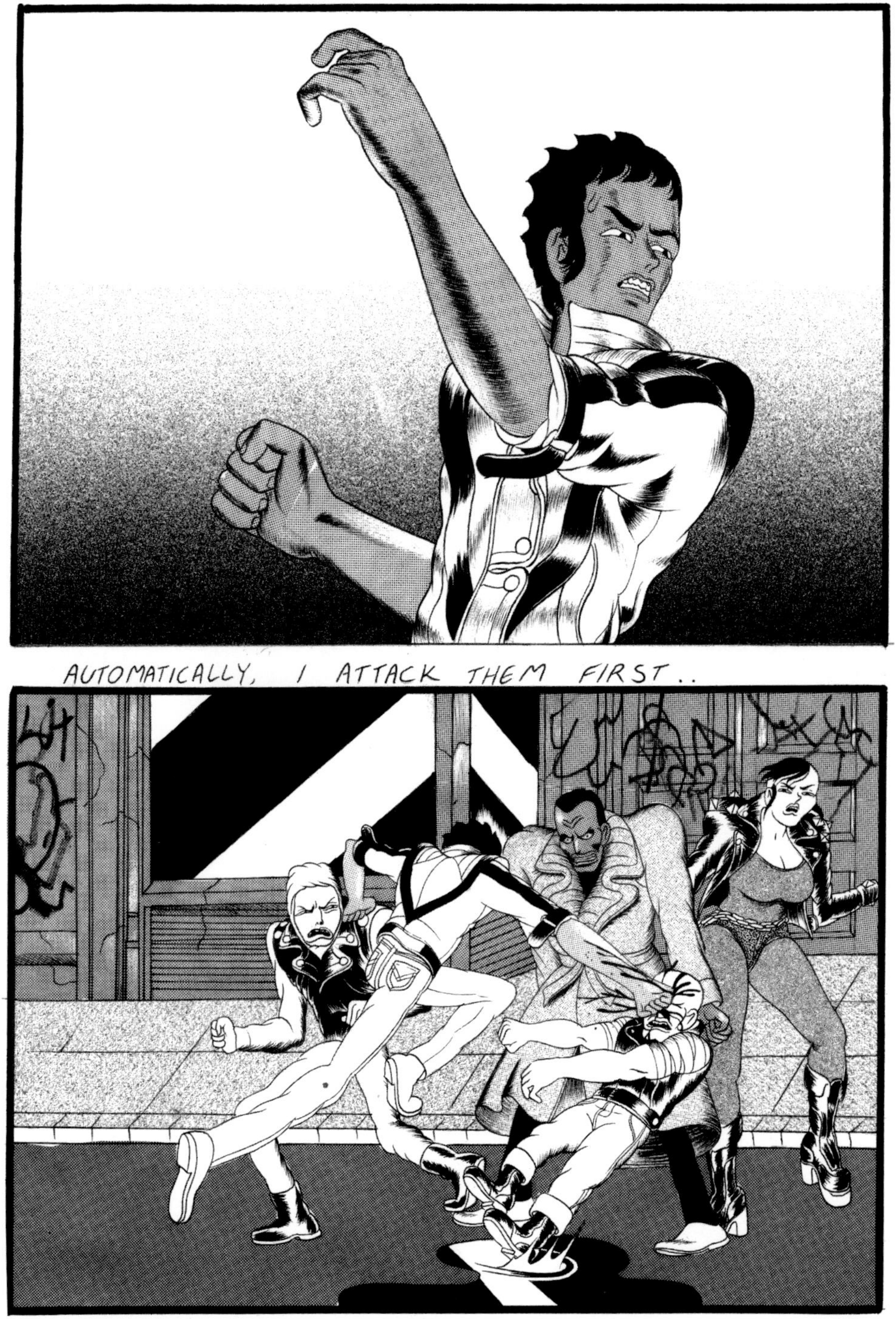
AUTOMATICALLY, I ATTACK THEM FIRST..

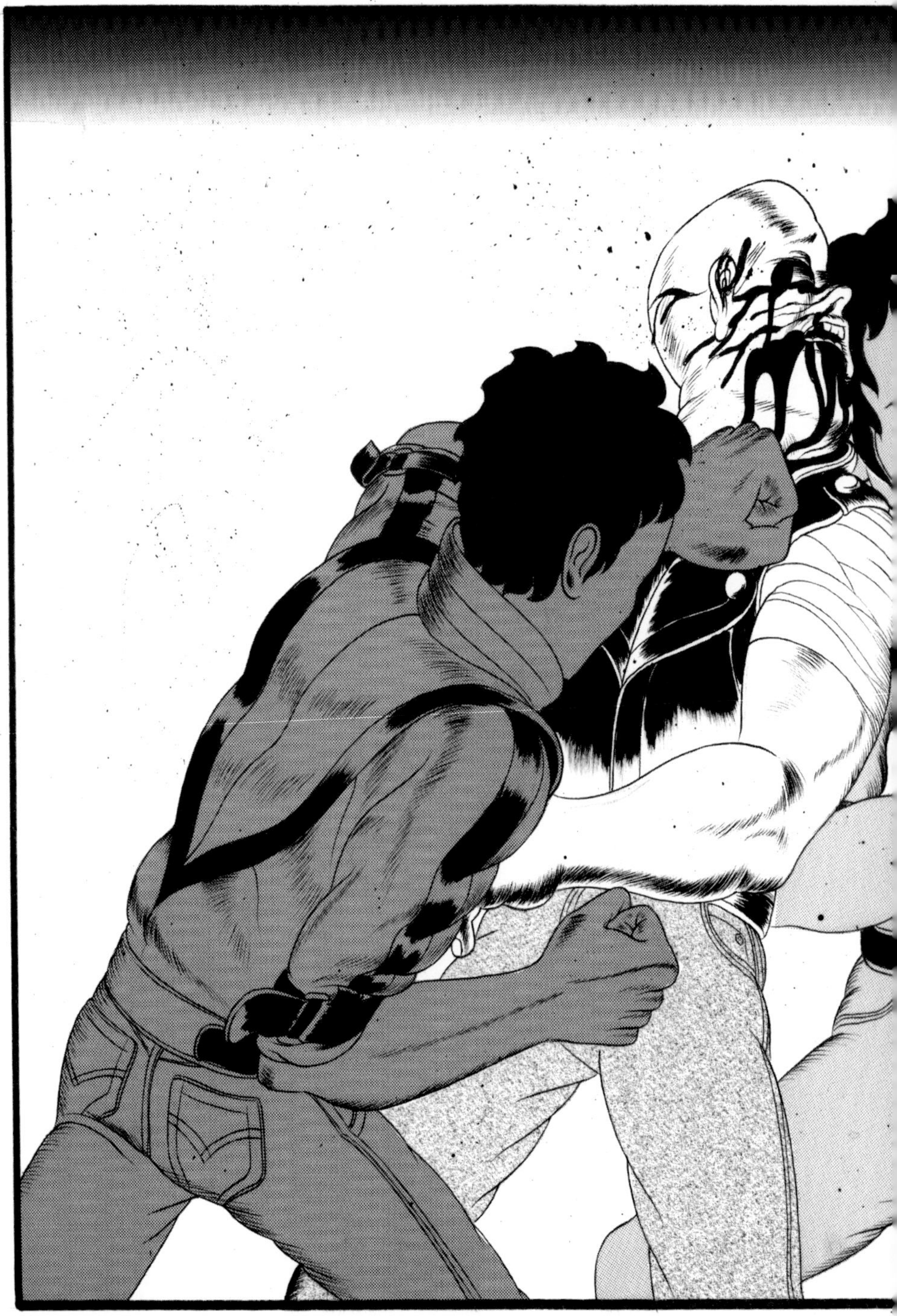

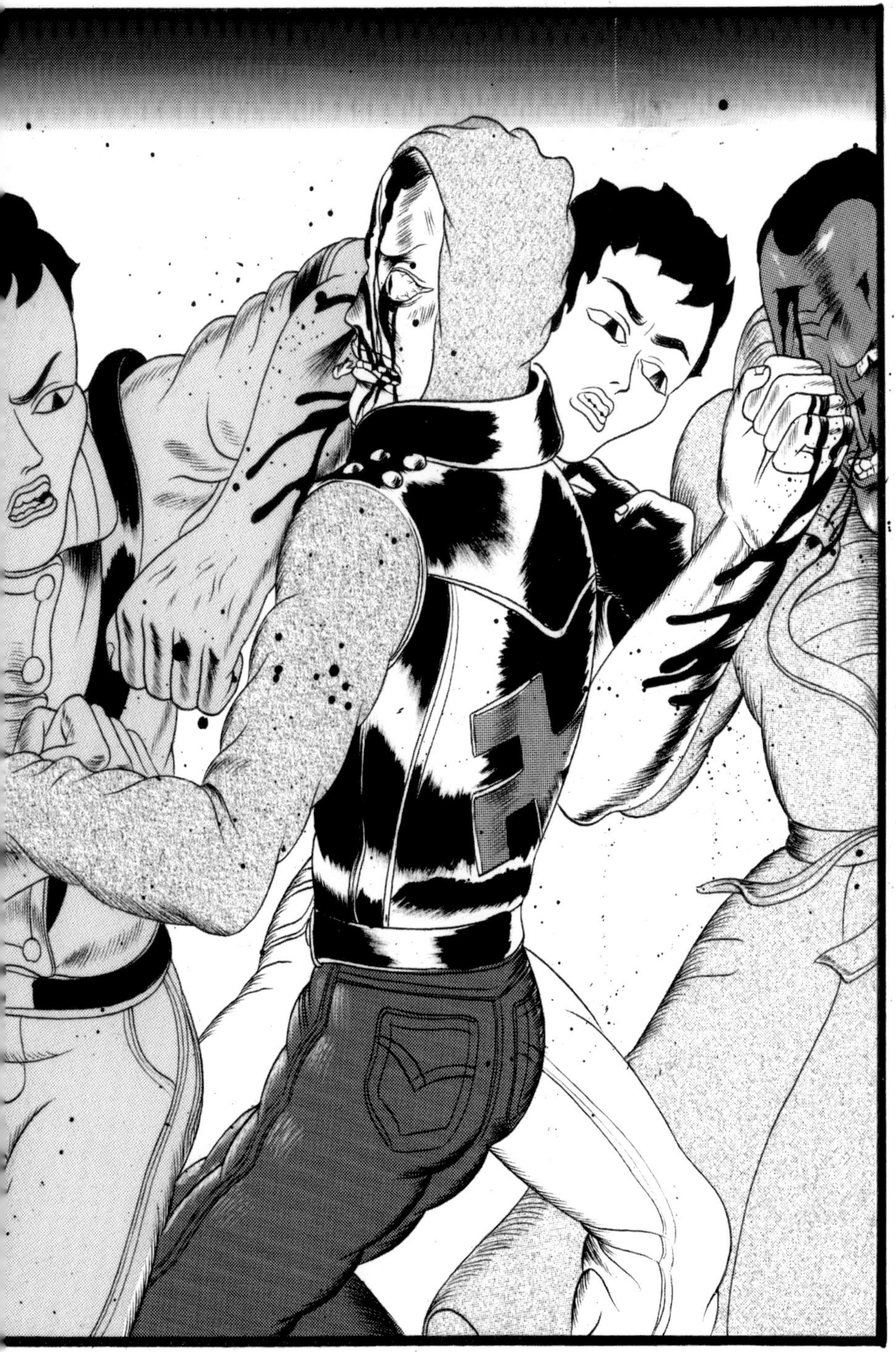

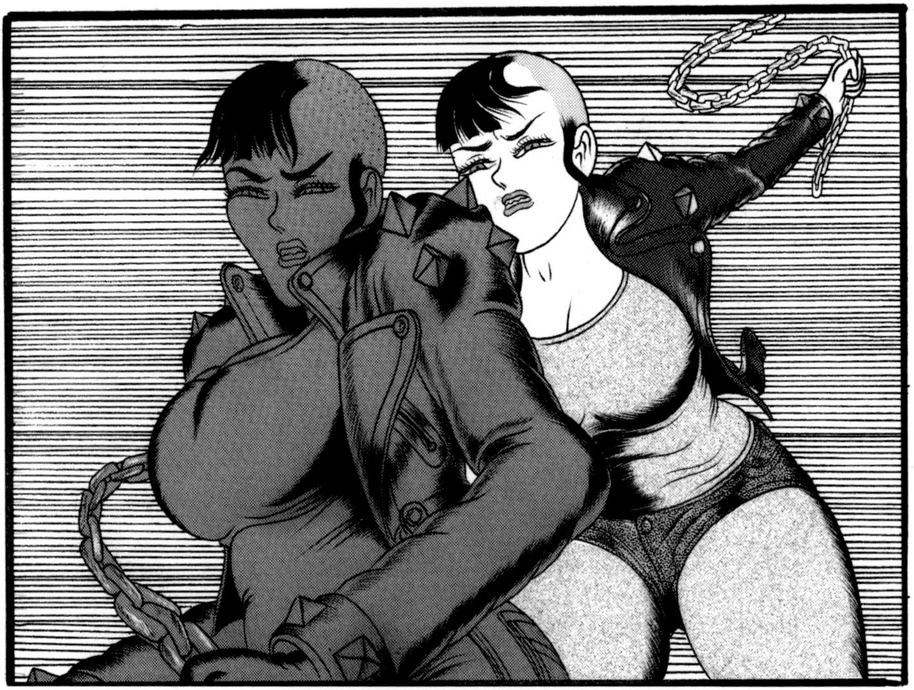

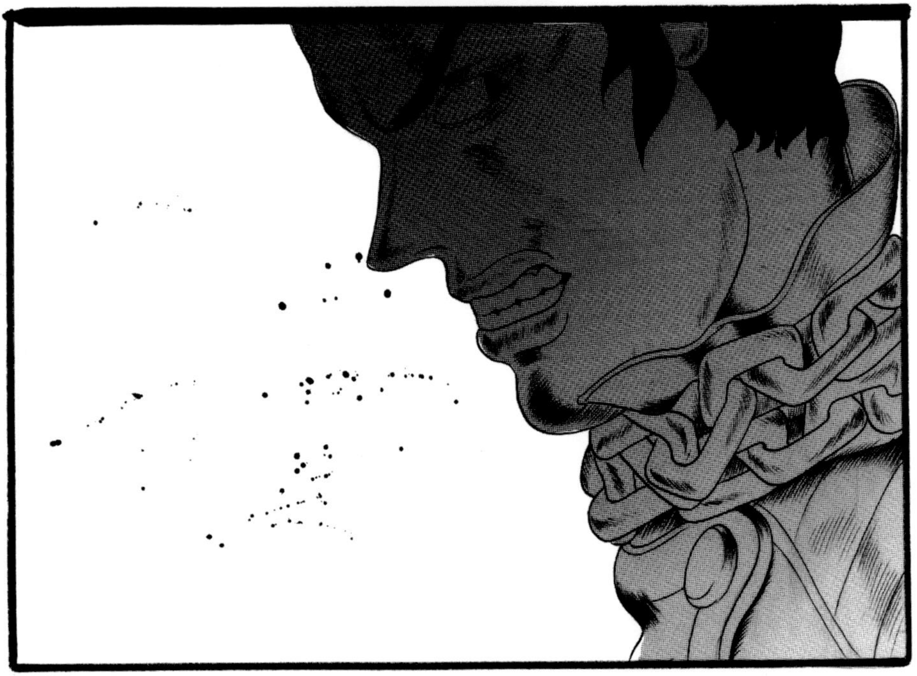

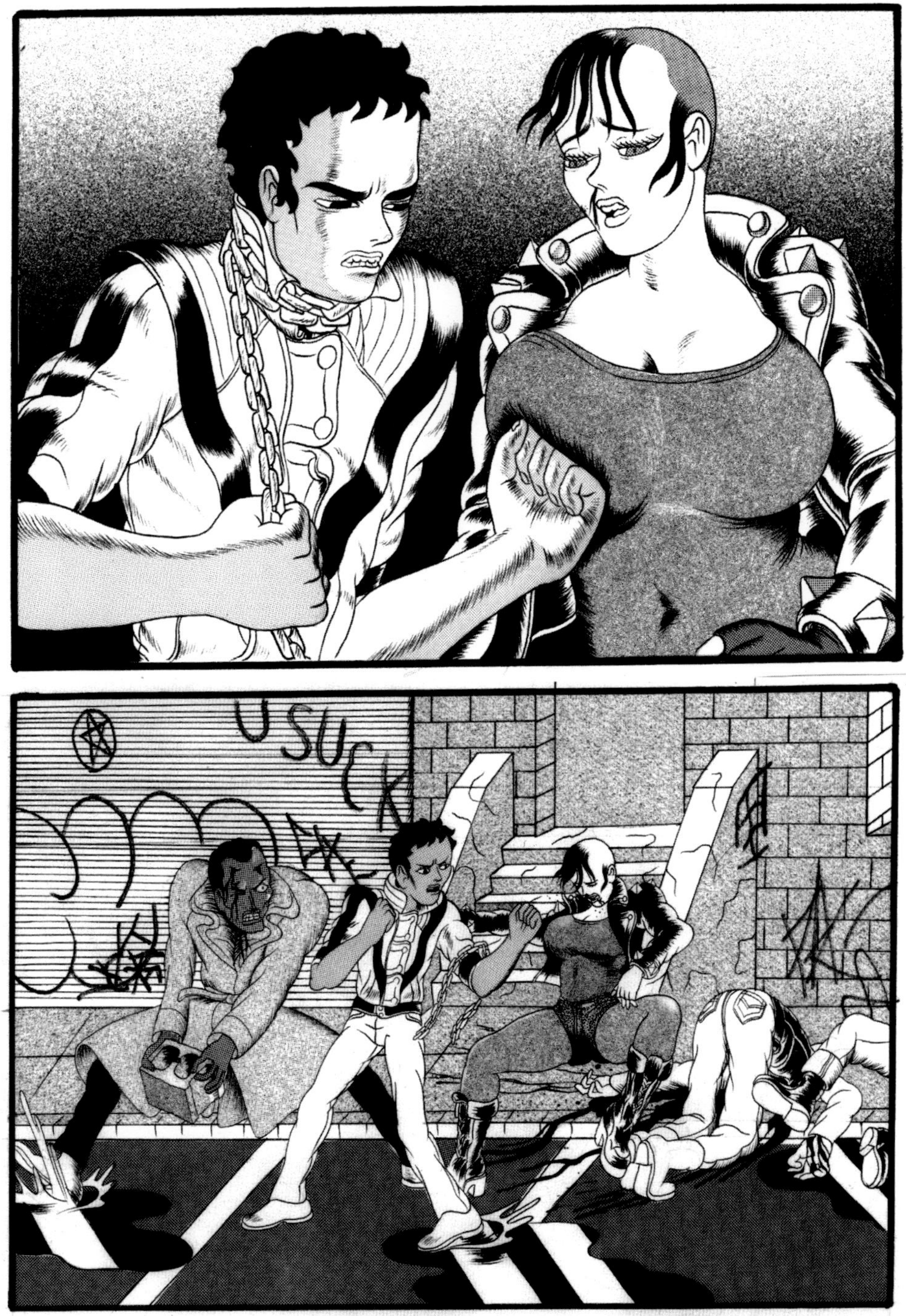
USUCK

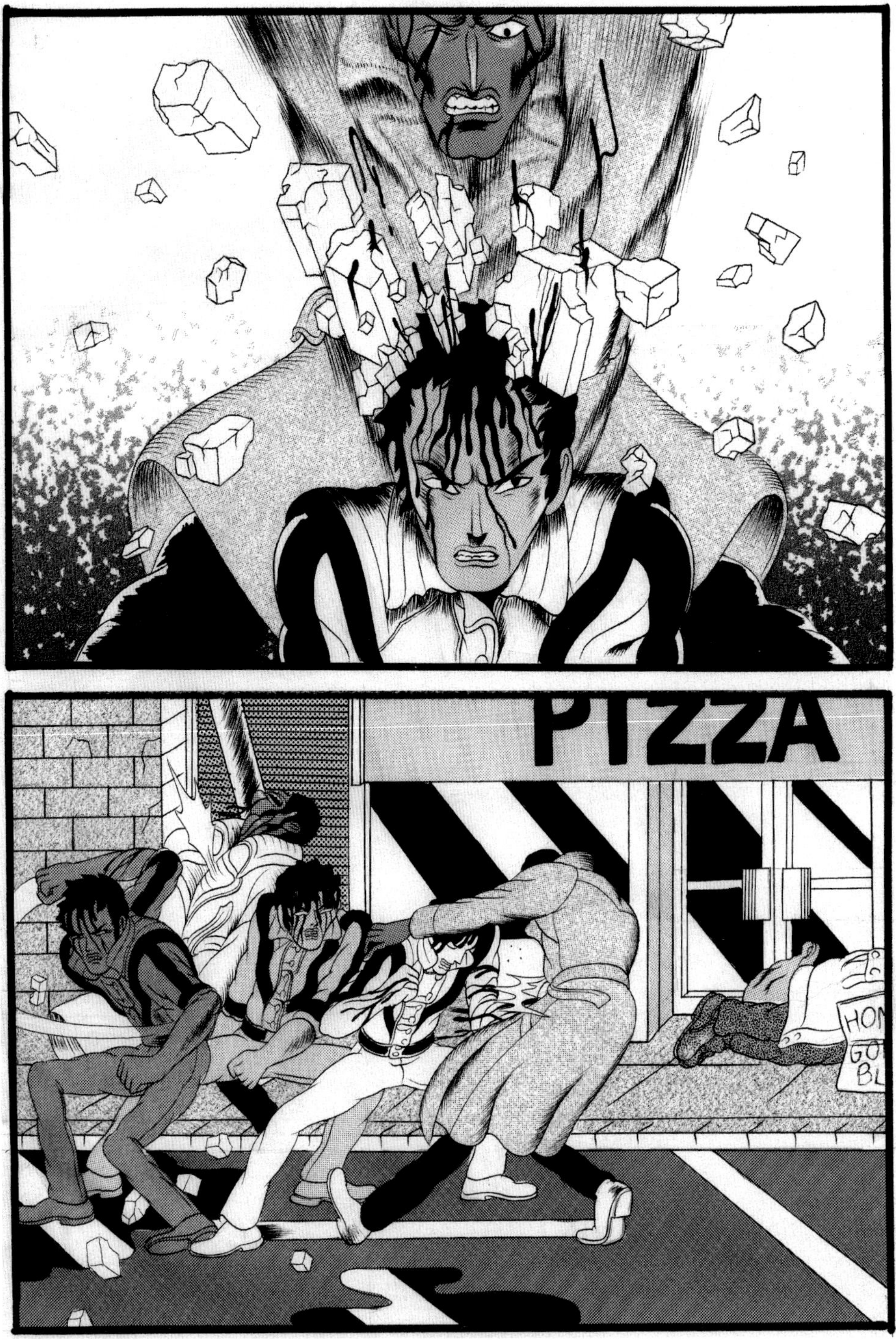
PIZZA

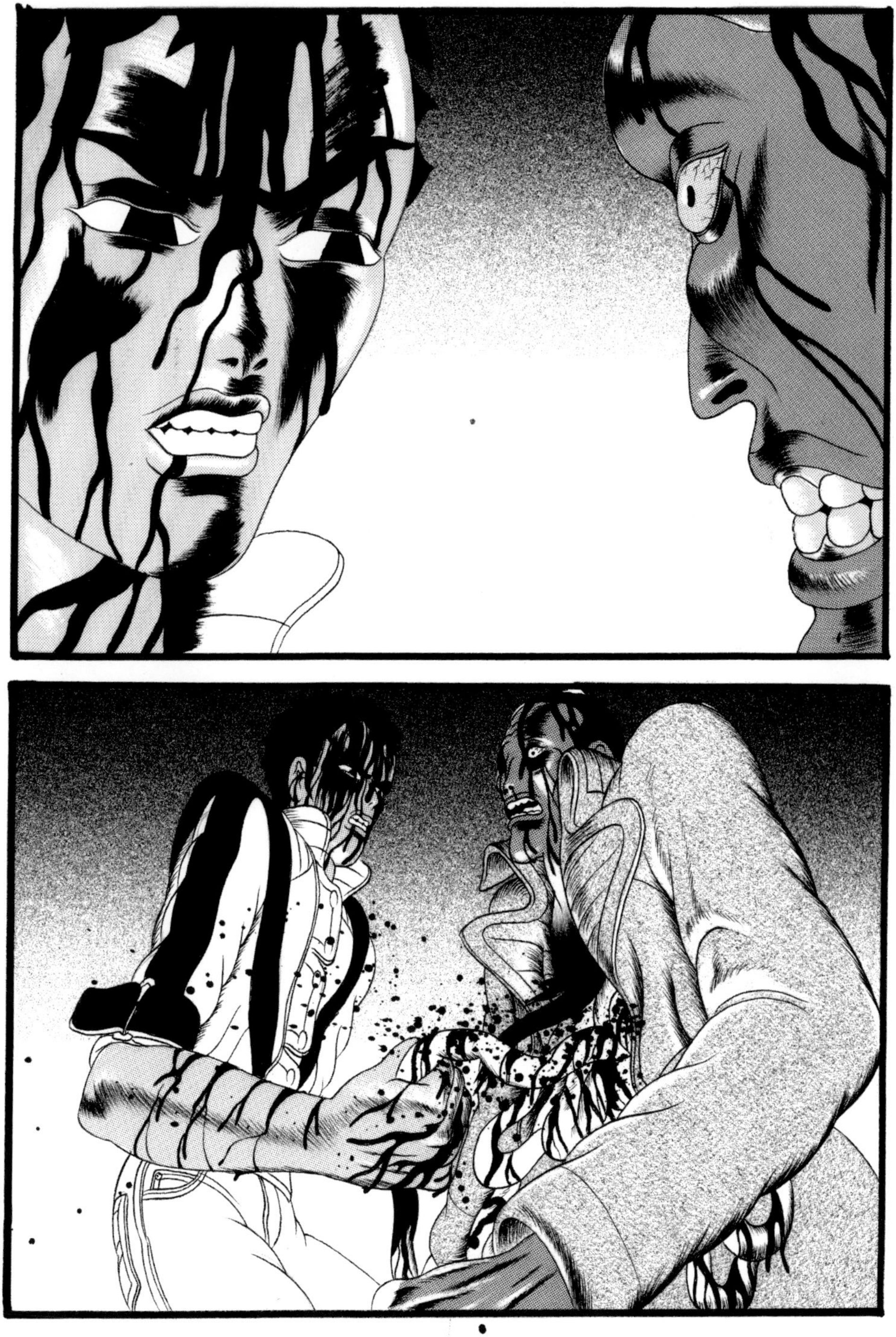

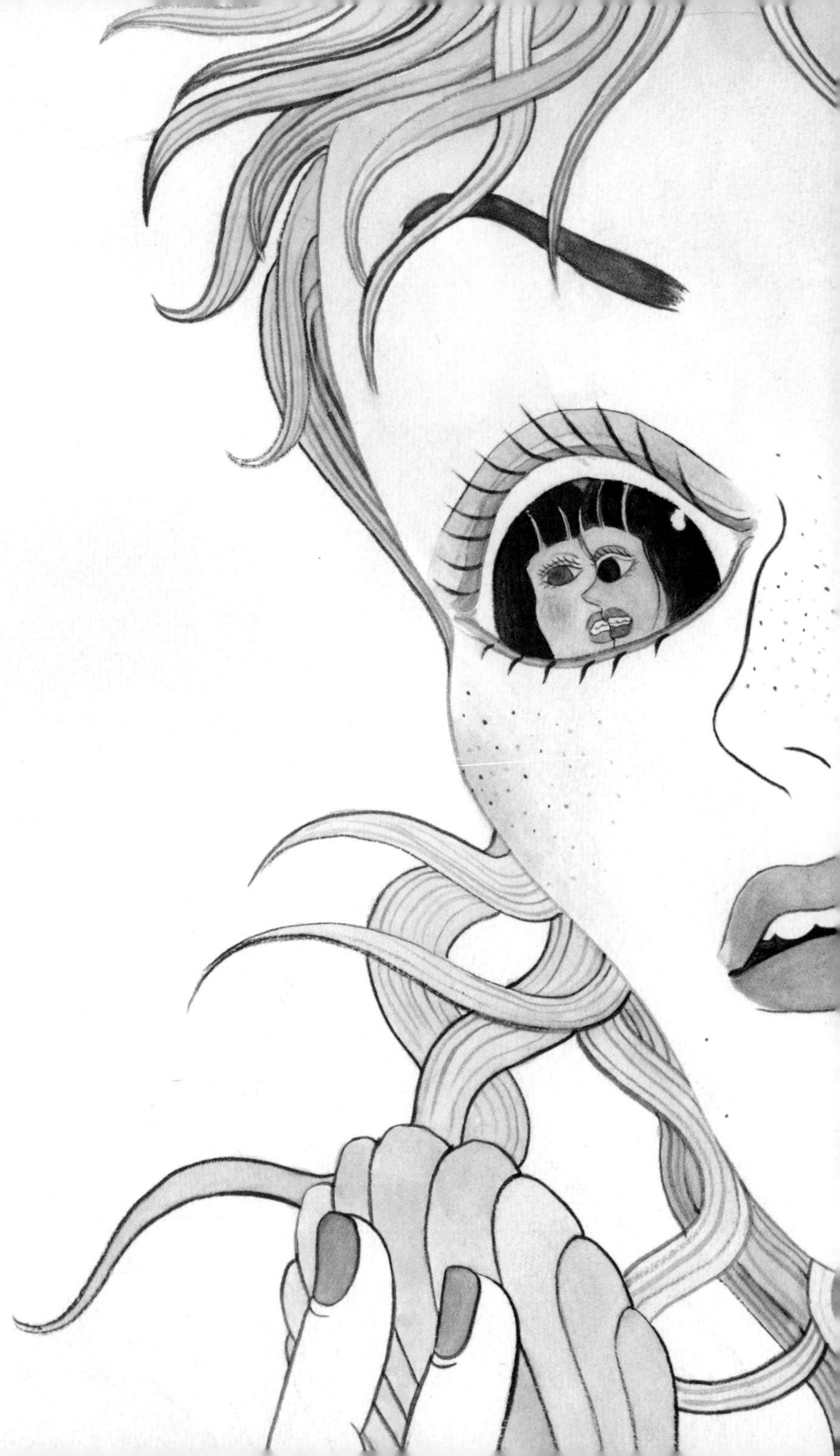

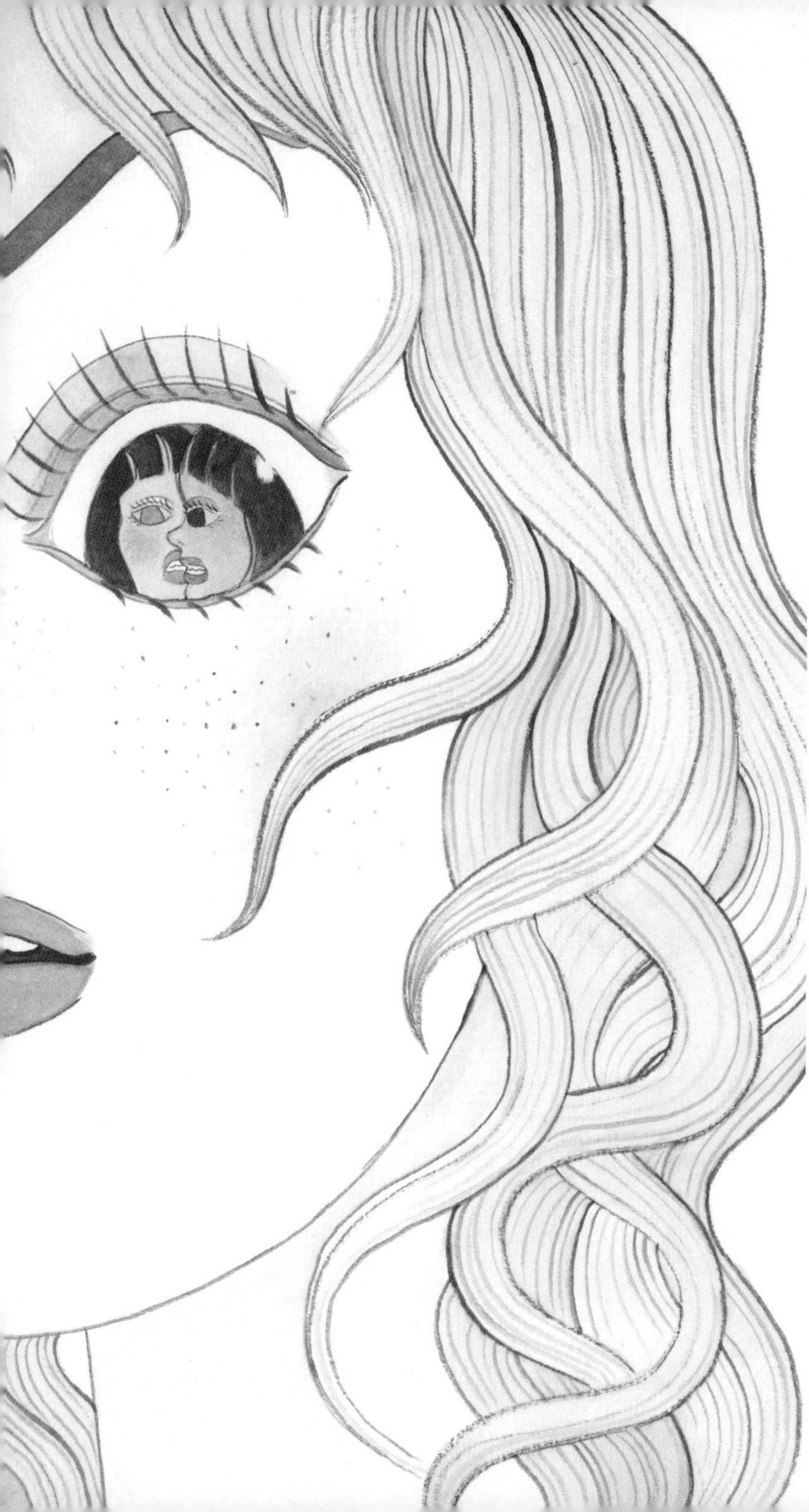

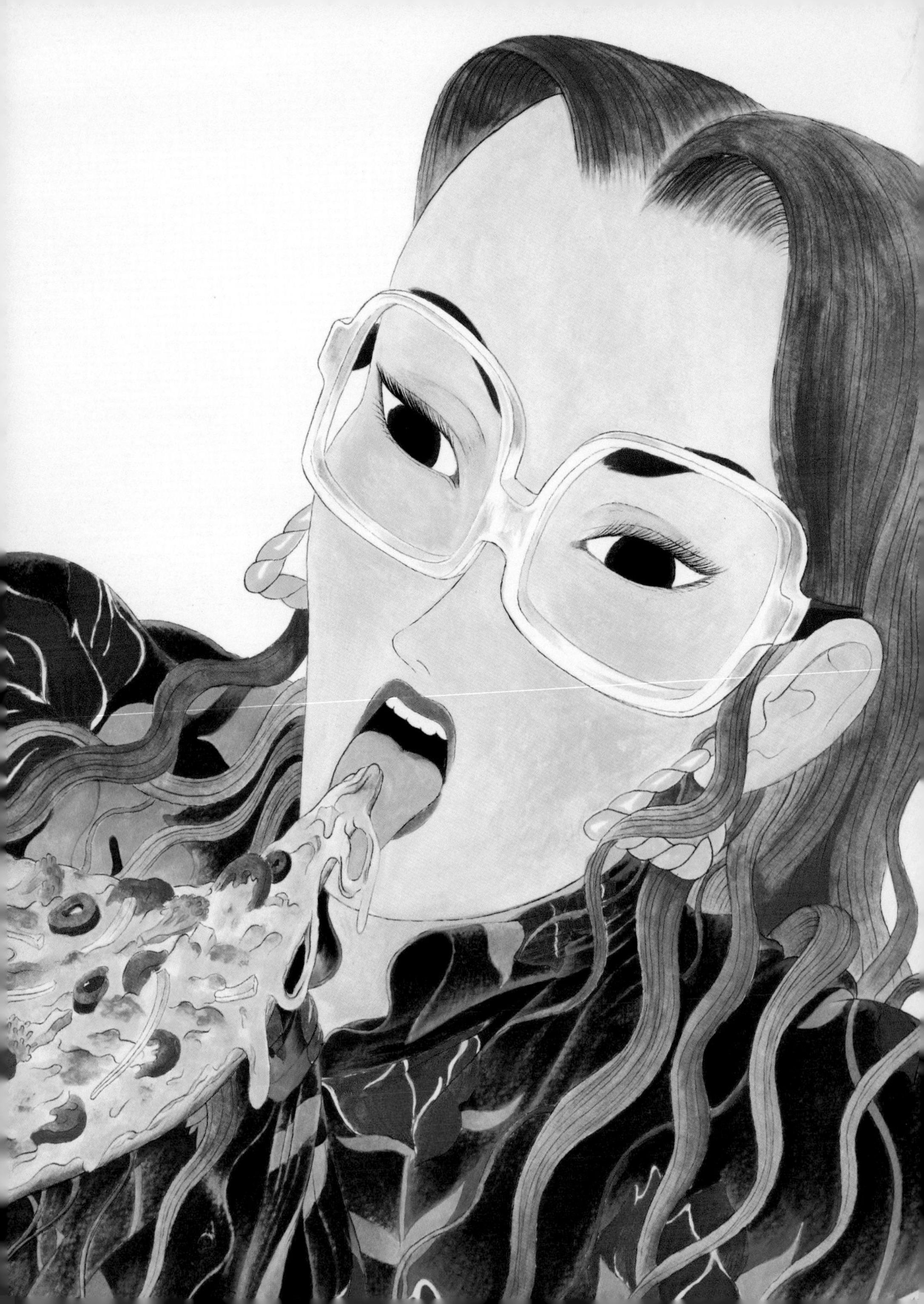

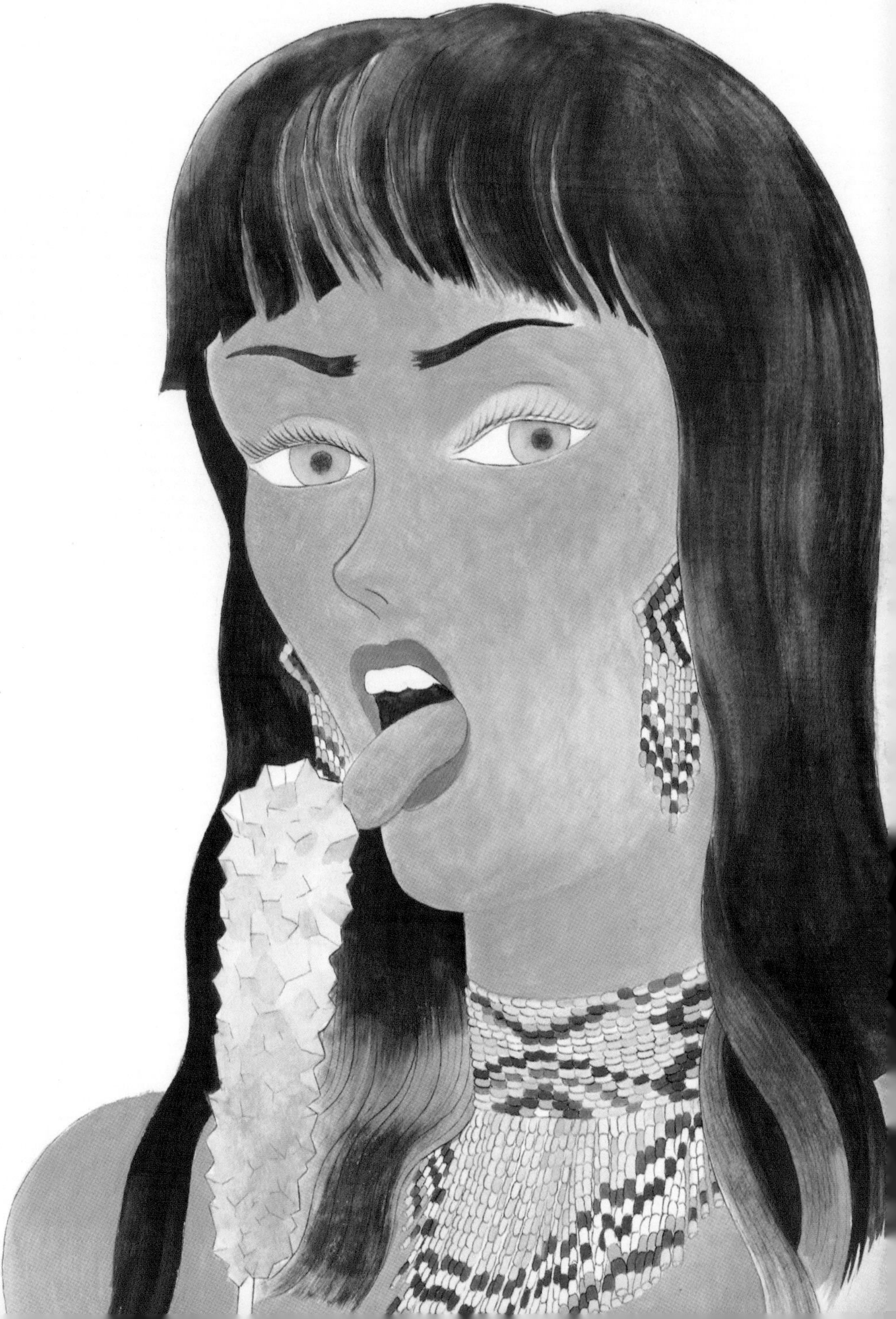

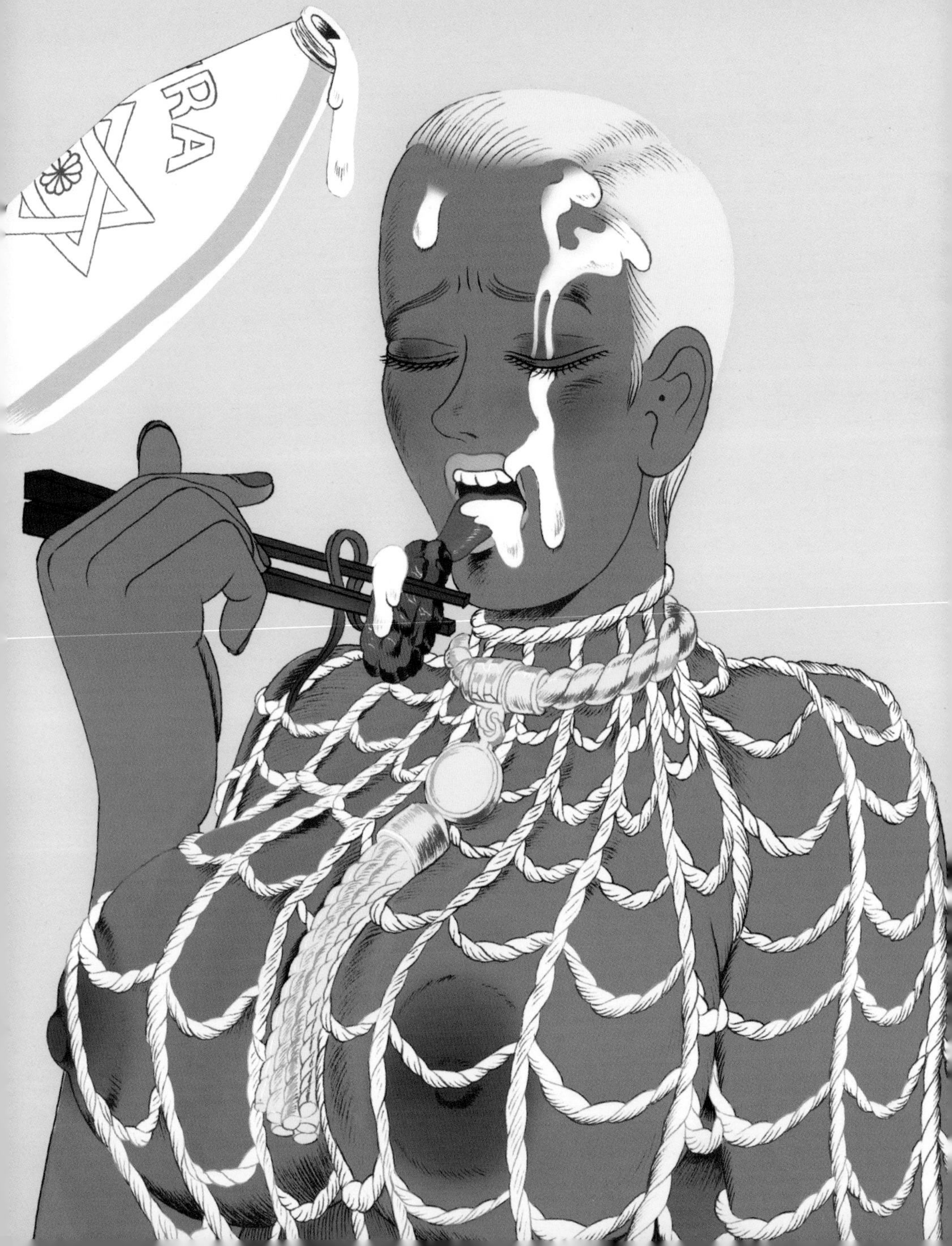

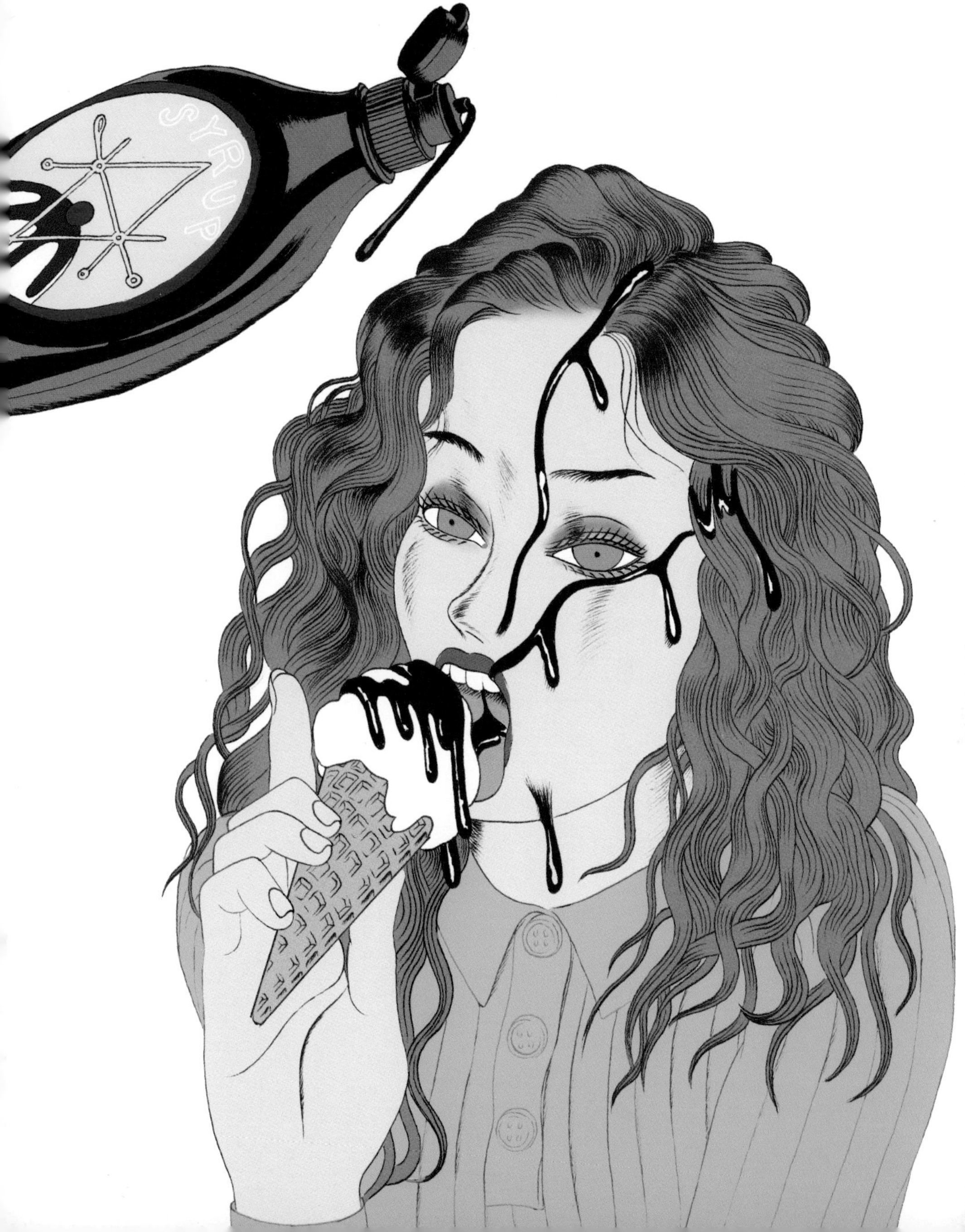
SYRUP

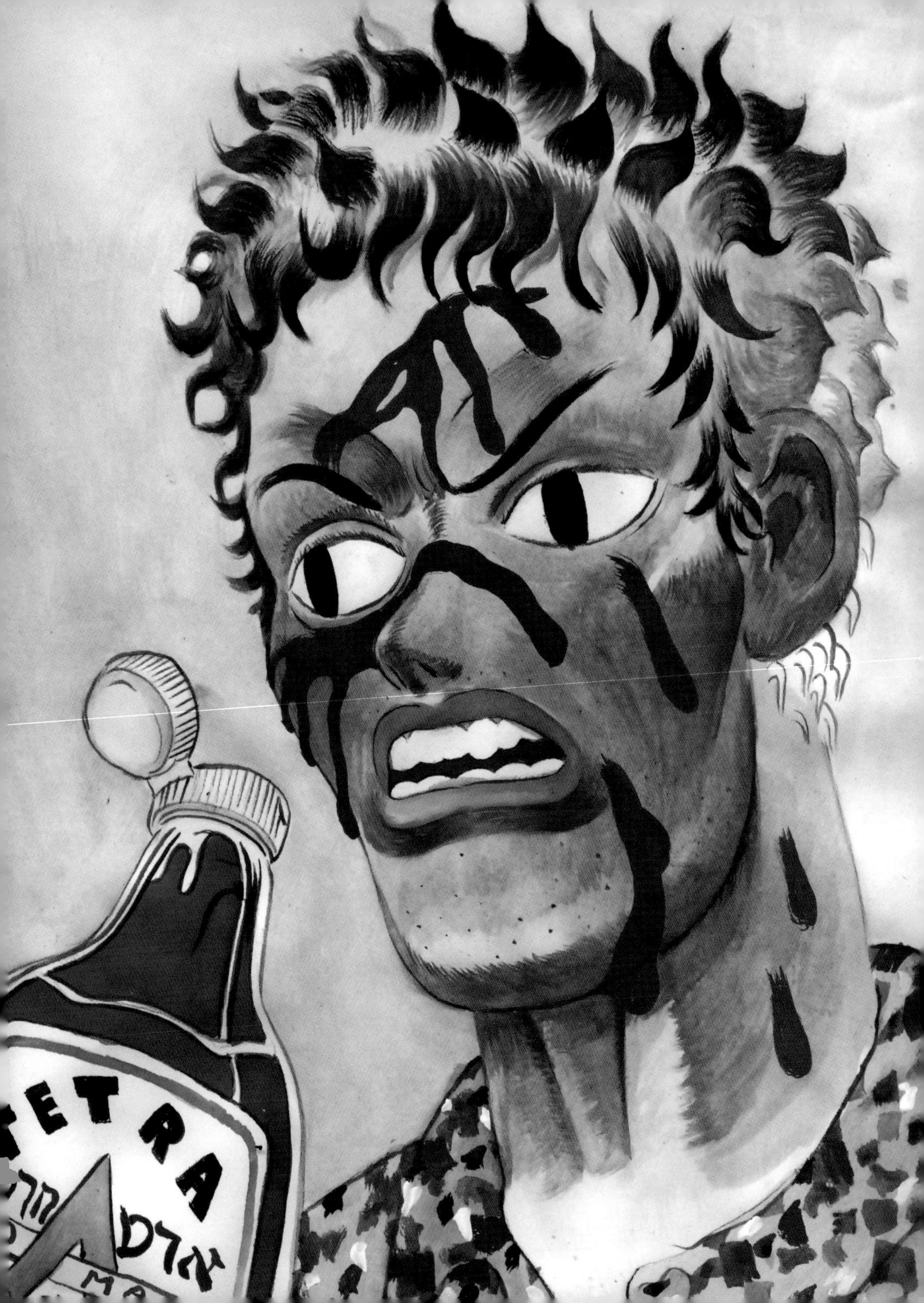
TETRA
אדם

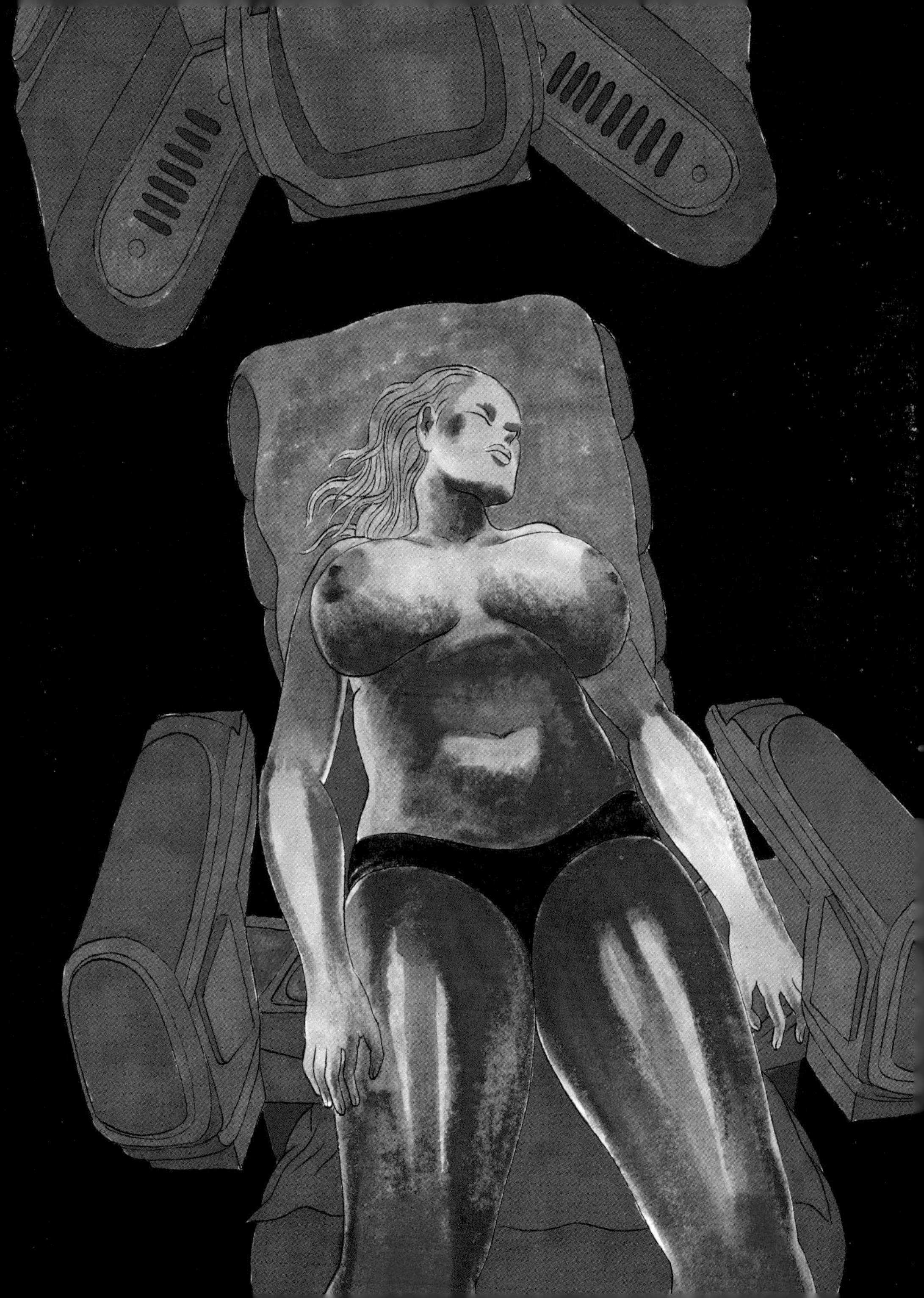

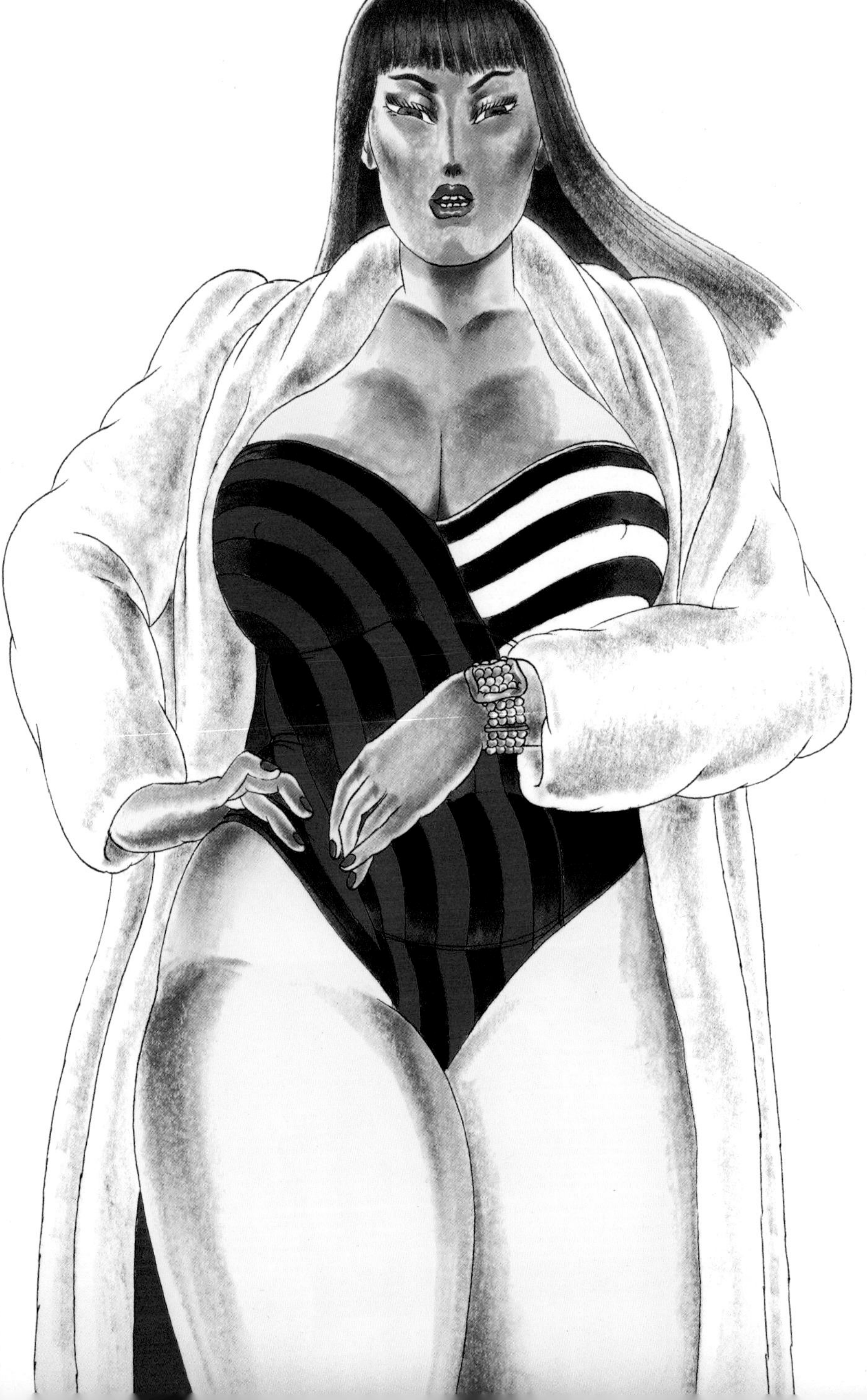

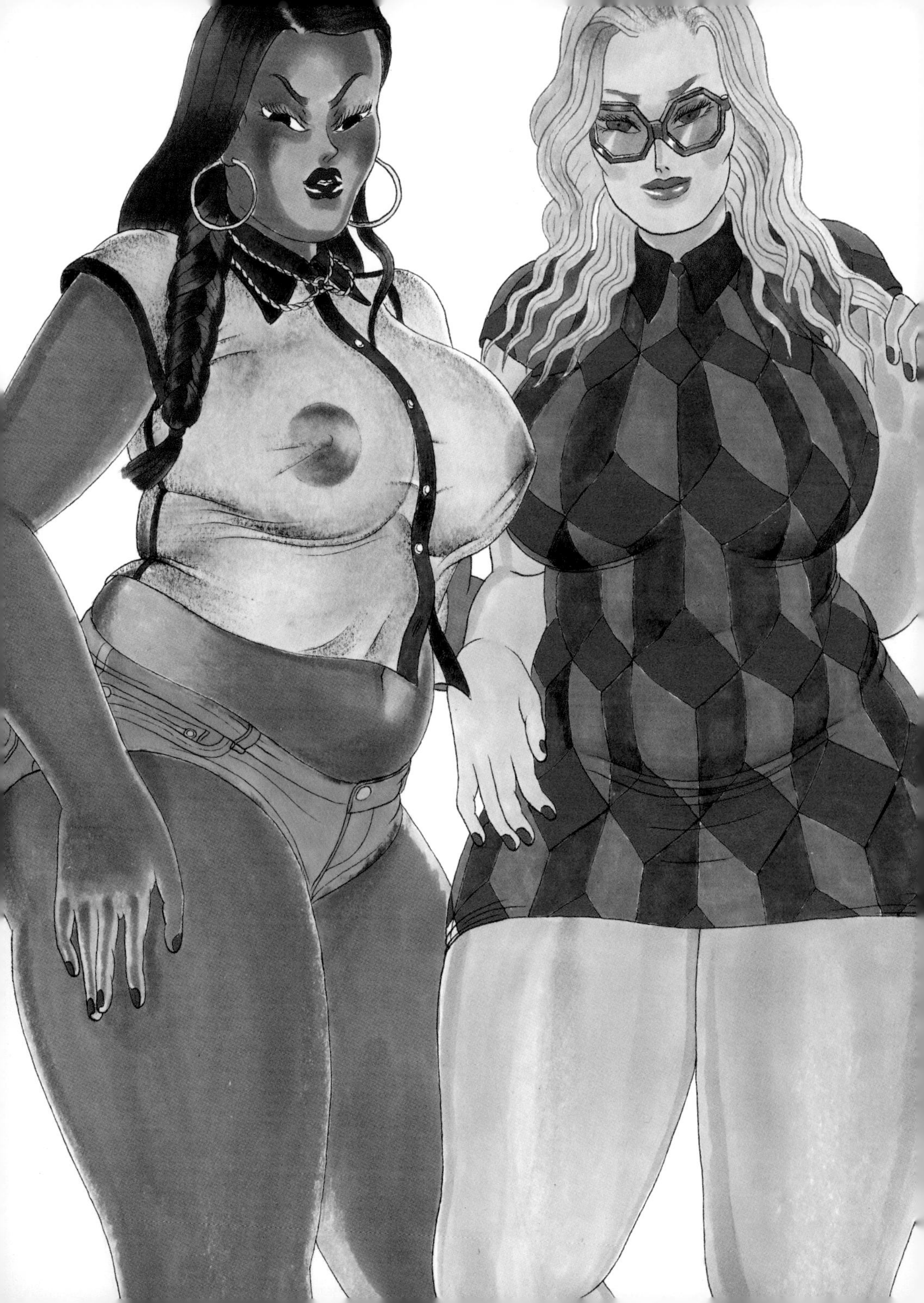

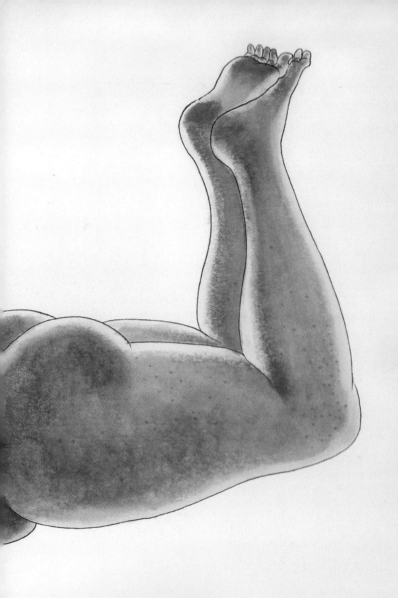

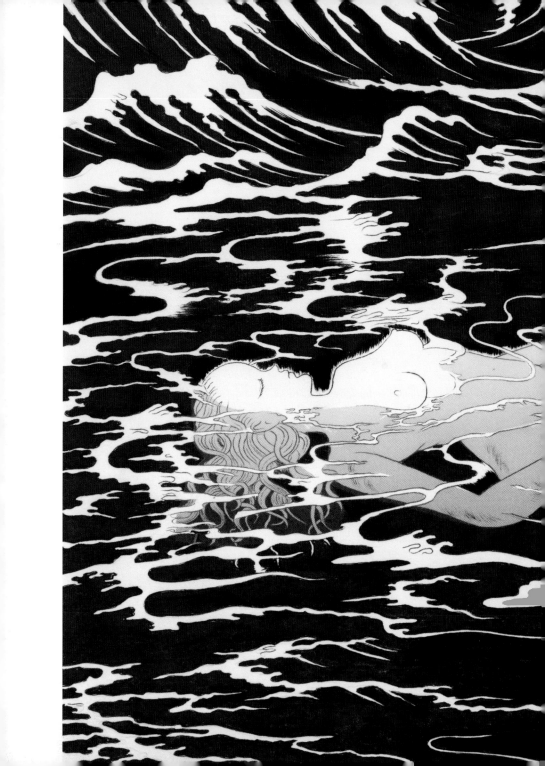

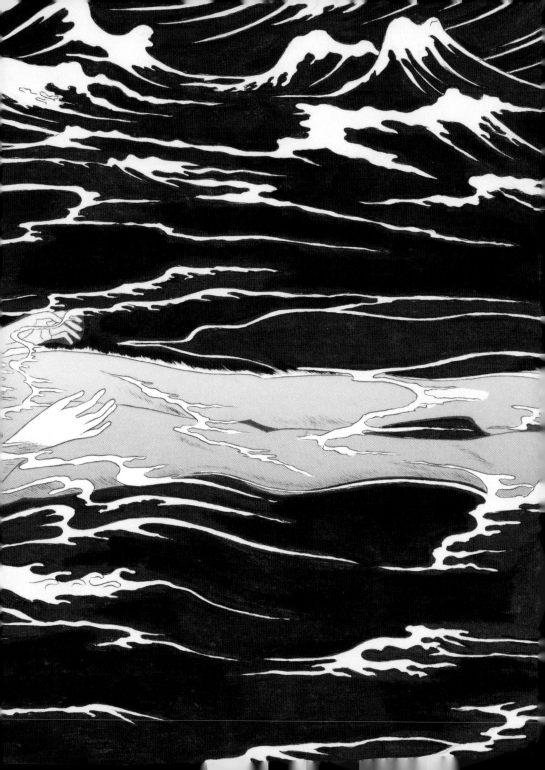

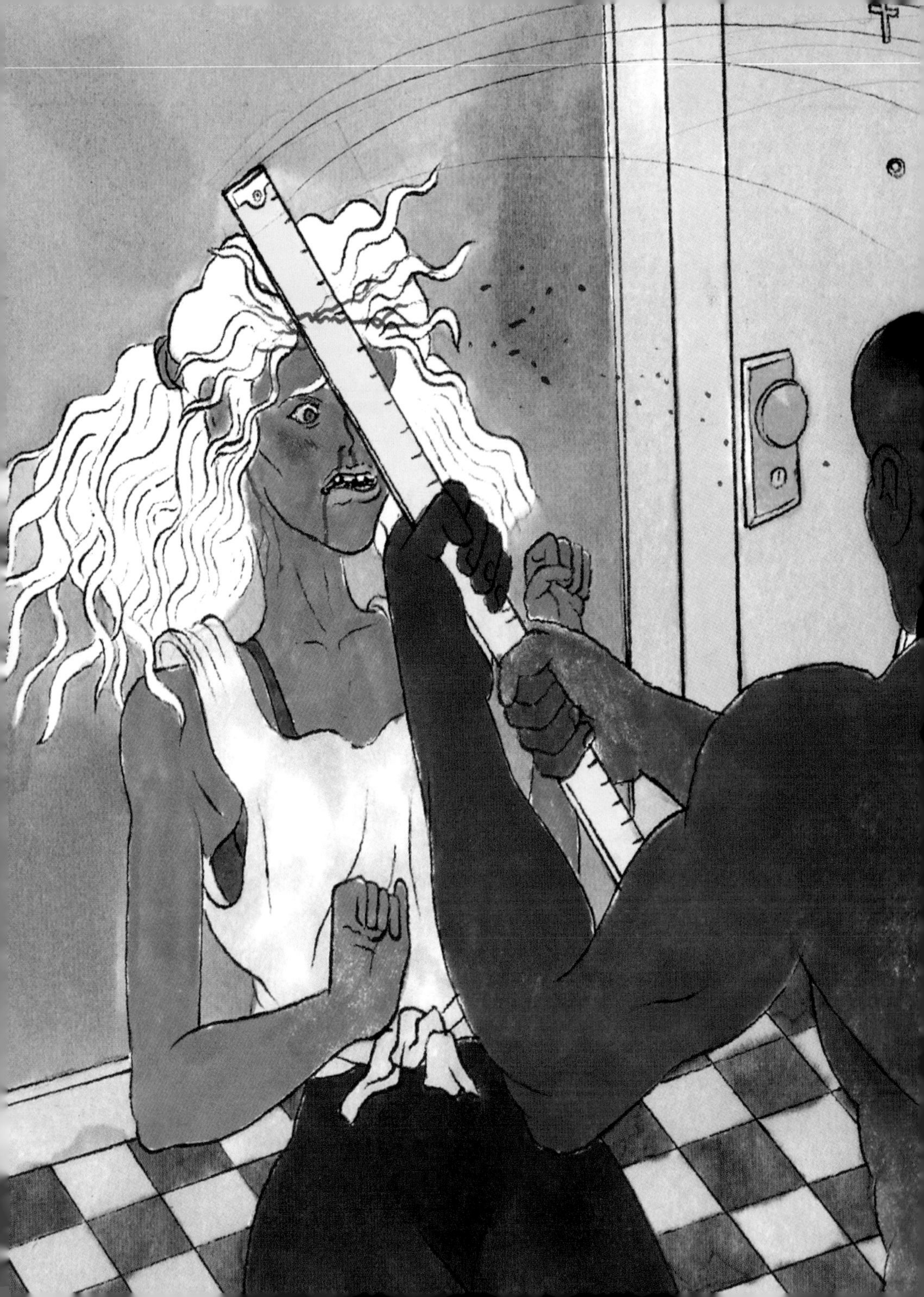

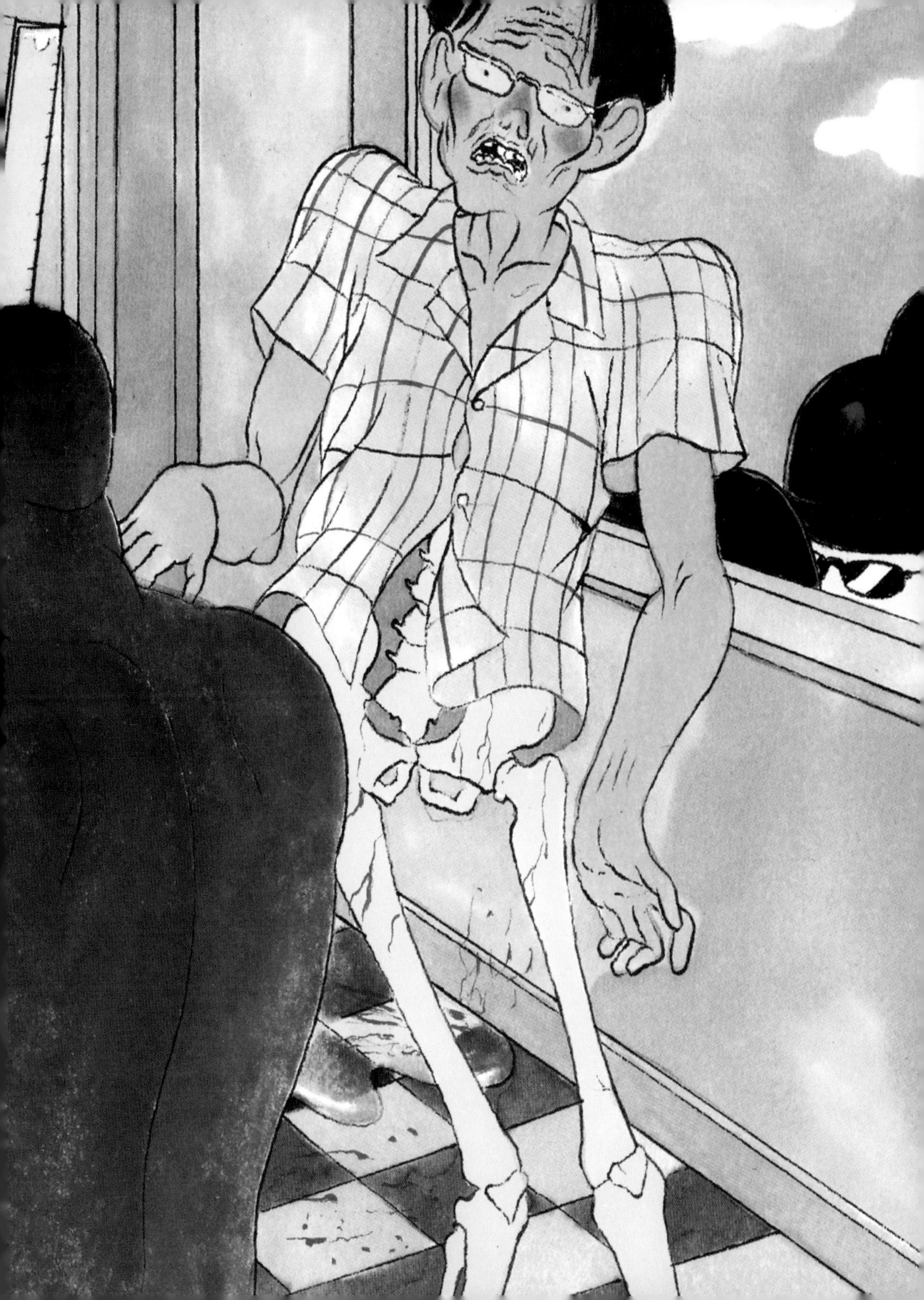

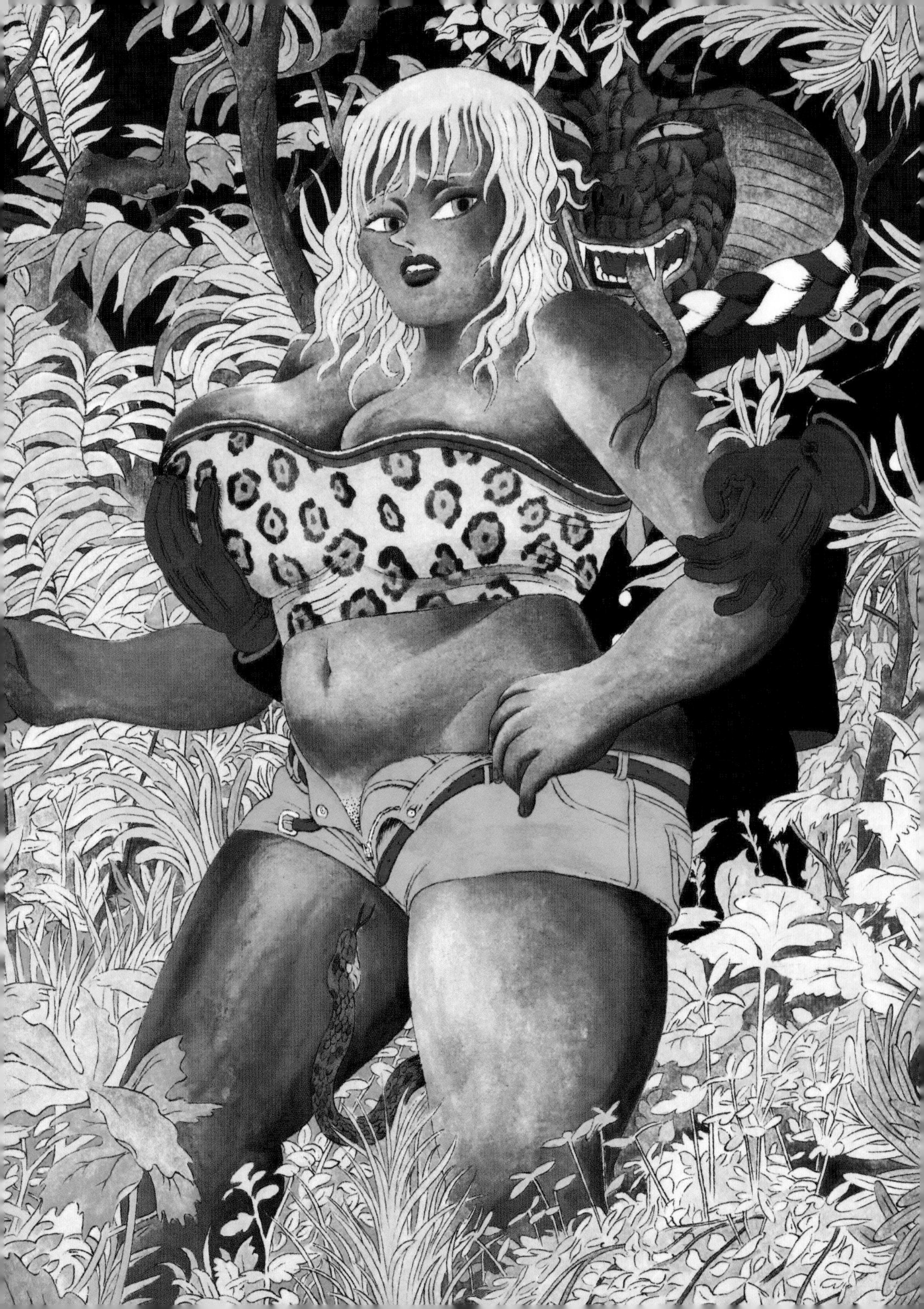

  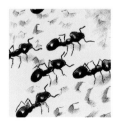 

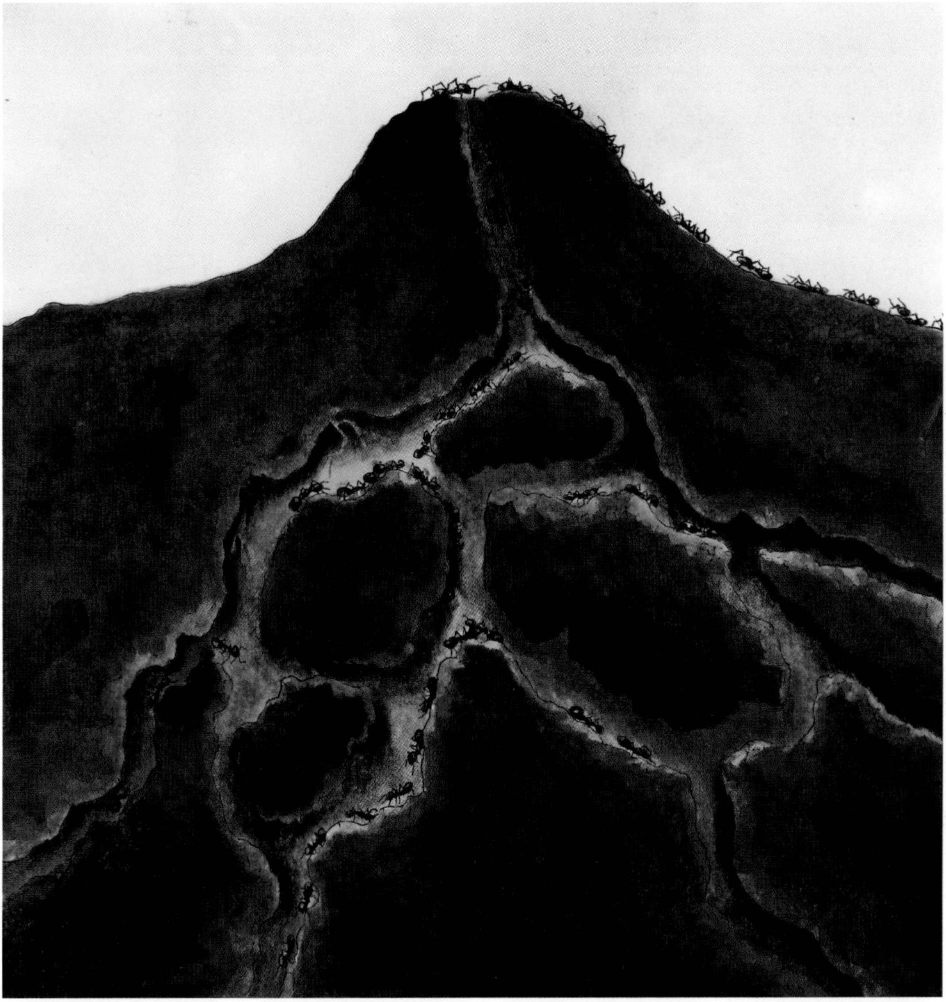
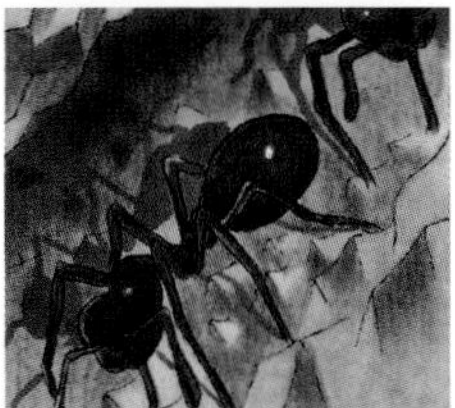
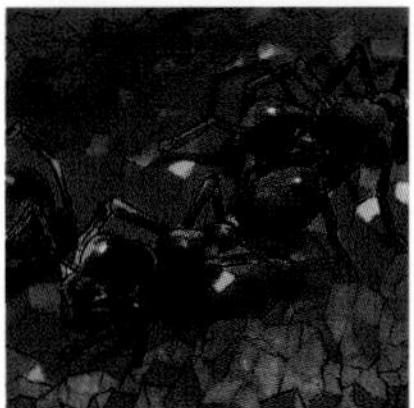
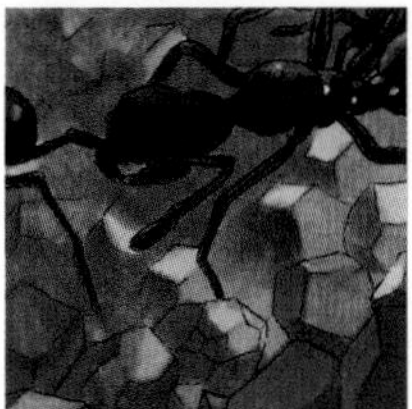
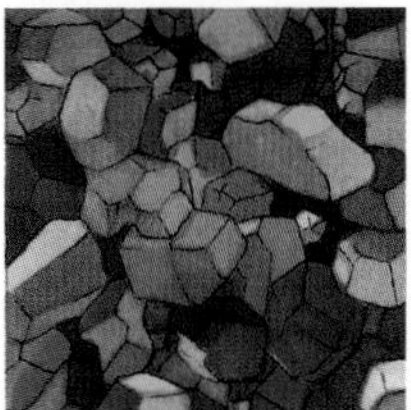

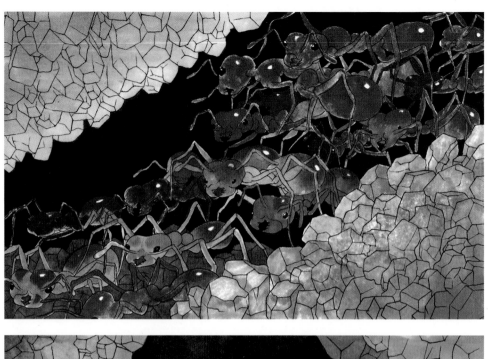
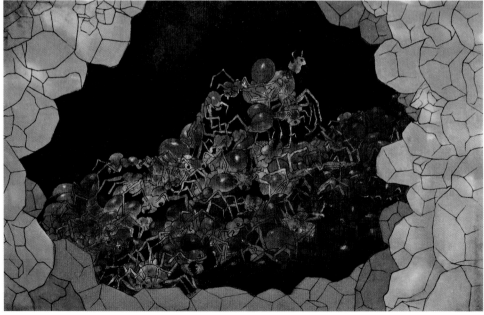

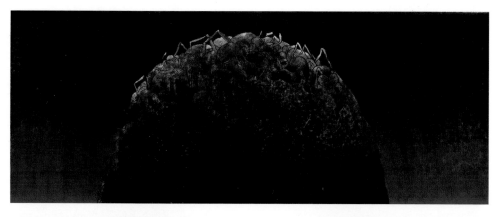

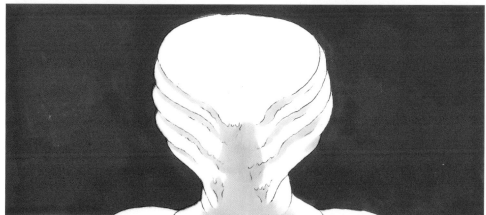

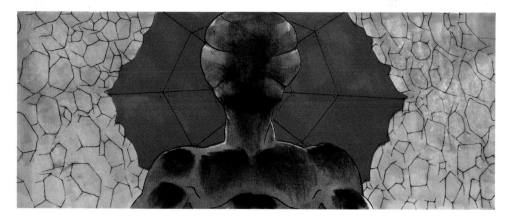

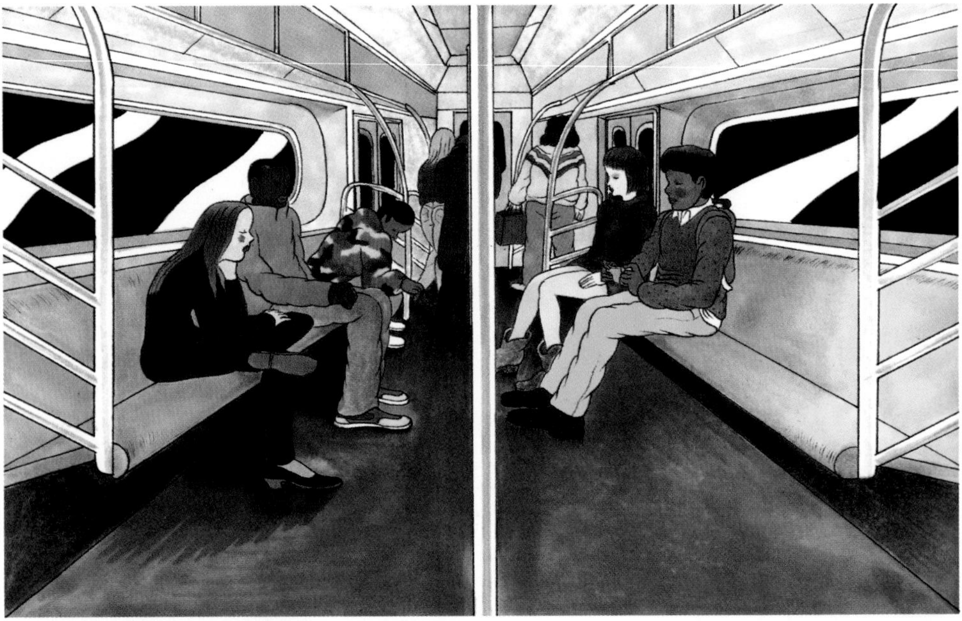

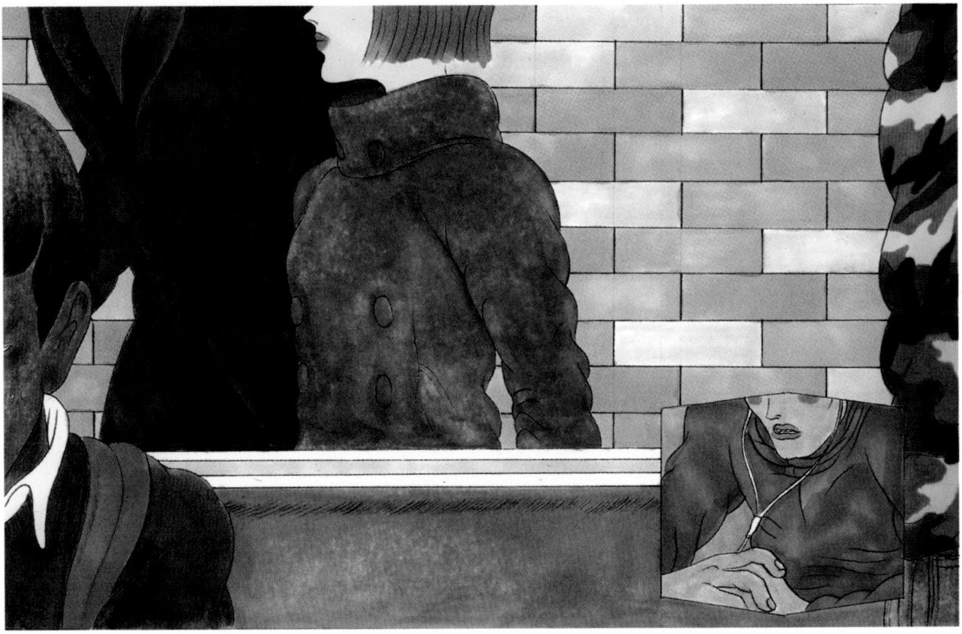

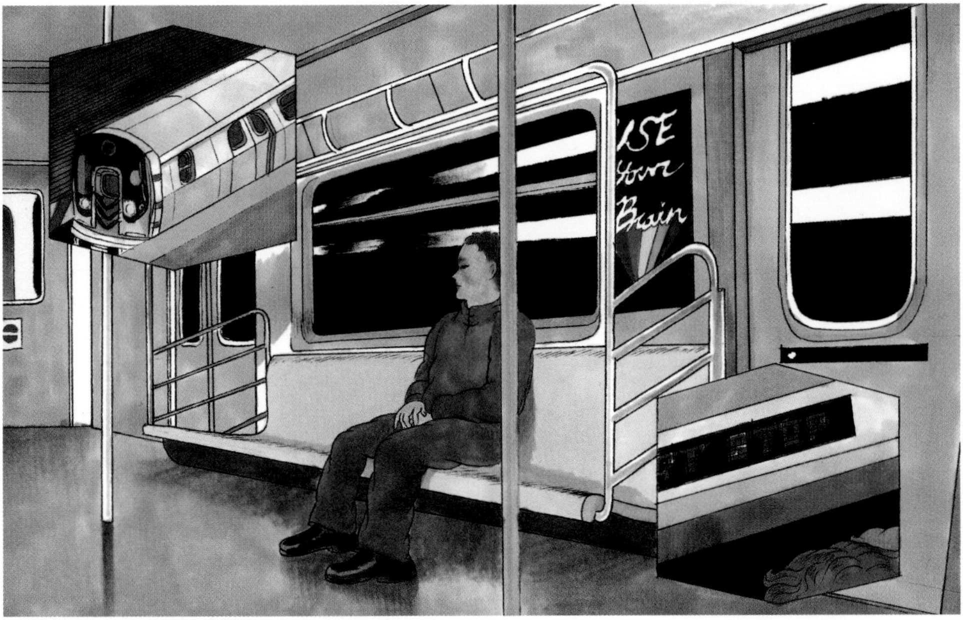
Your
Brain

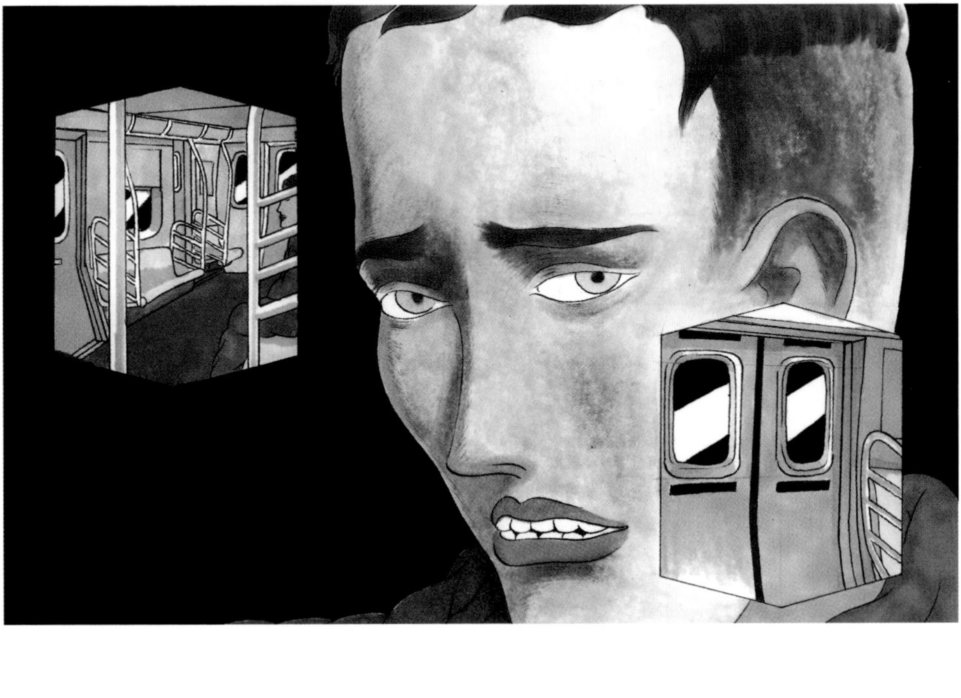

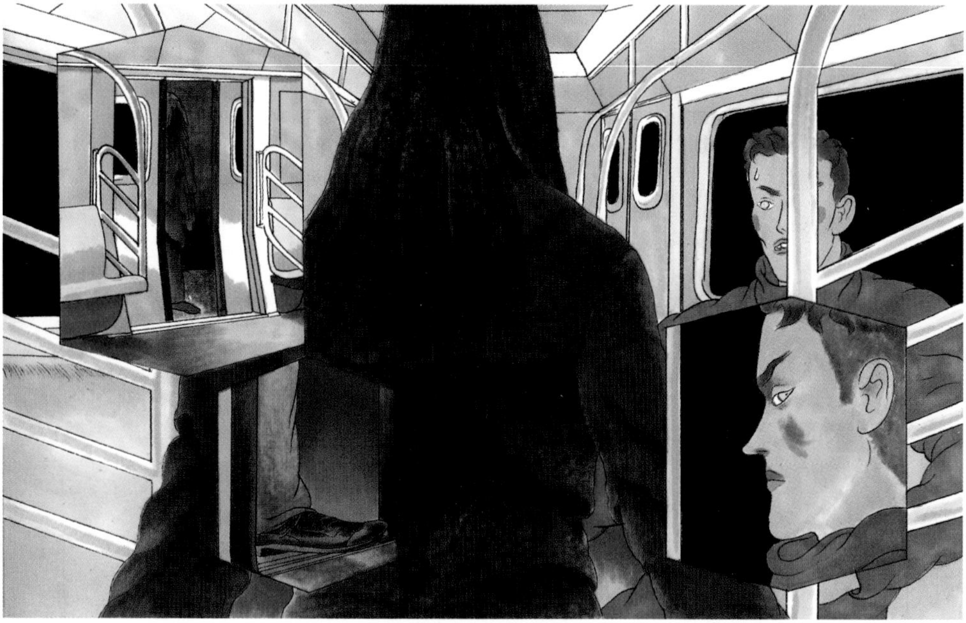

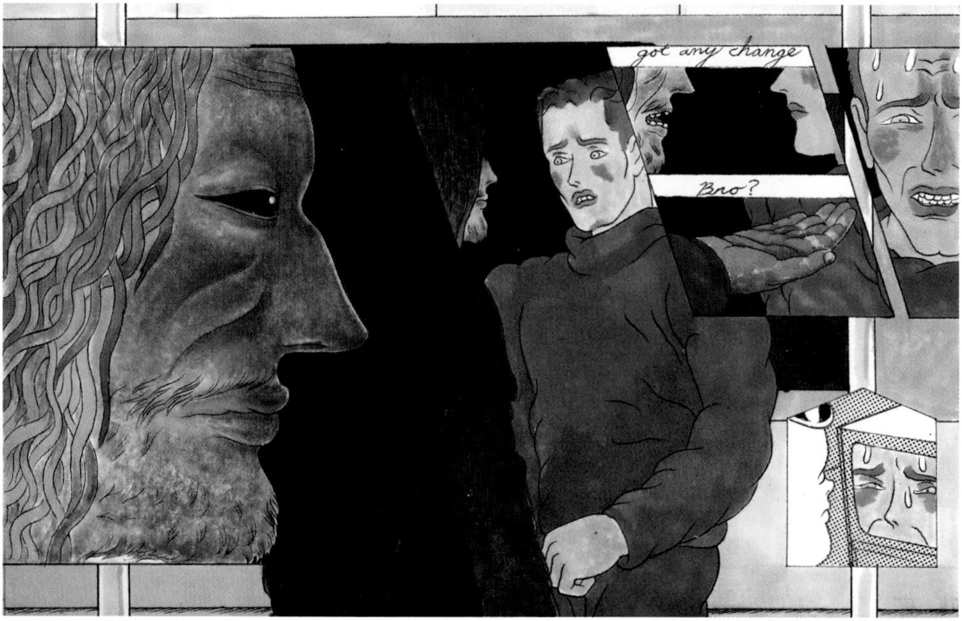
got any change
Bro?

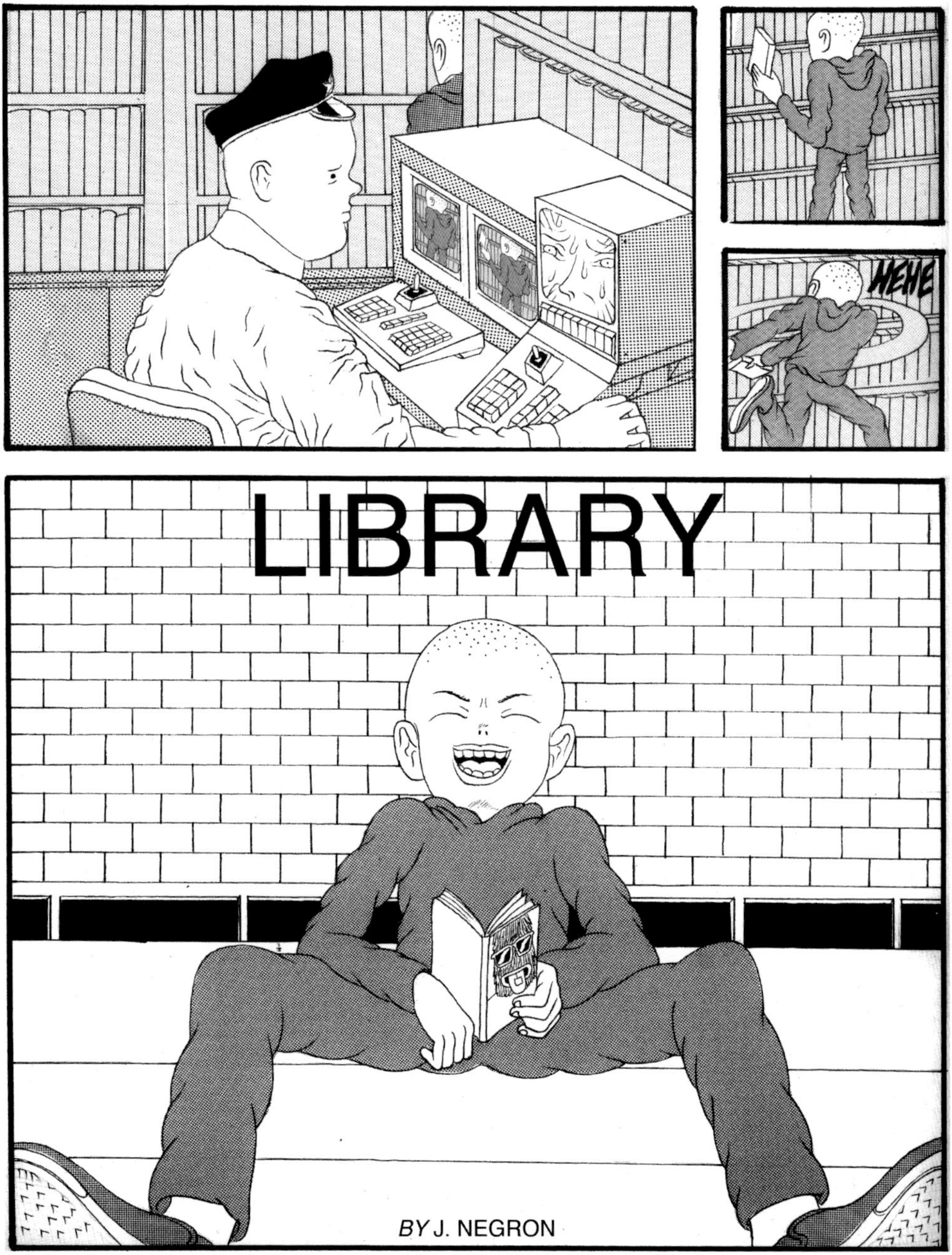
HEHE
LIBRARY
BY J. NEGRON

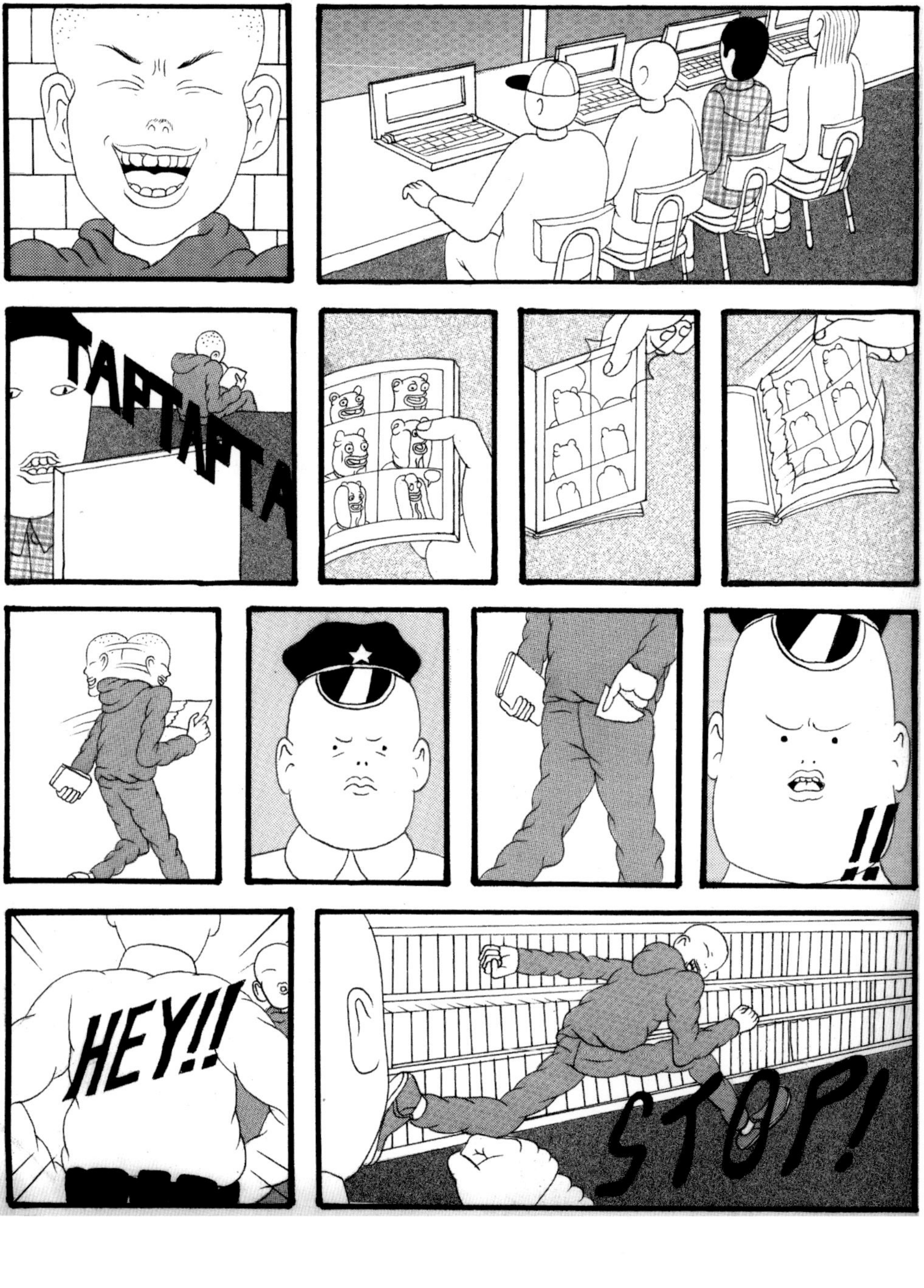
TAFTAFTA
!!
HEY!!
STOP!

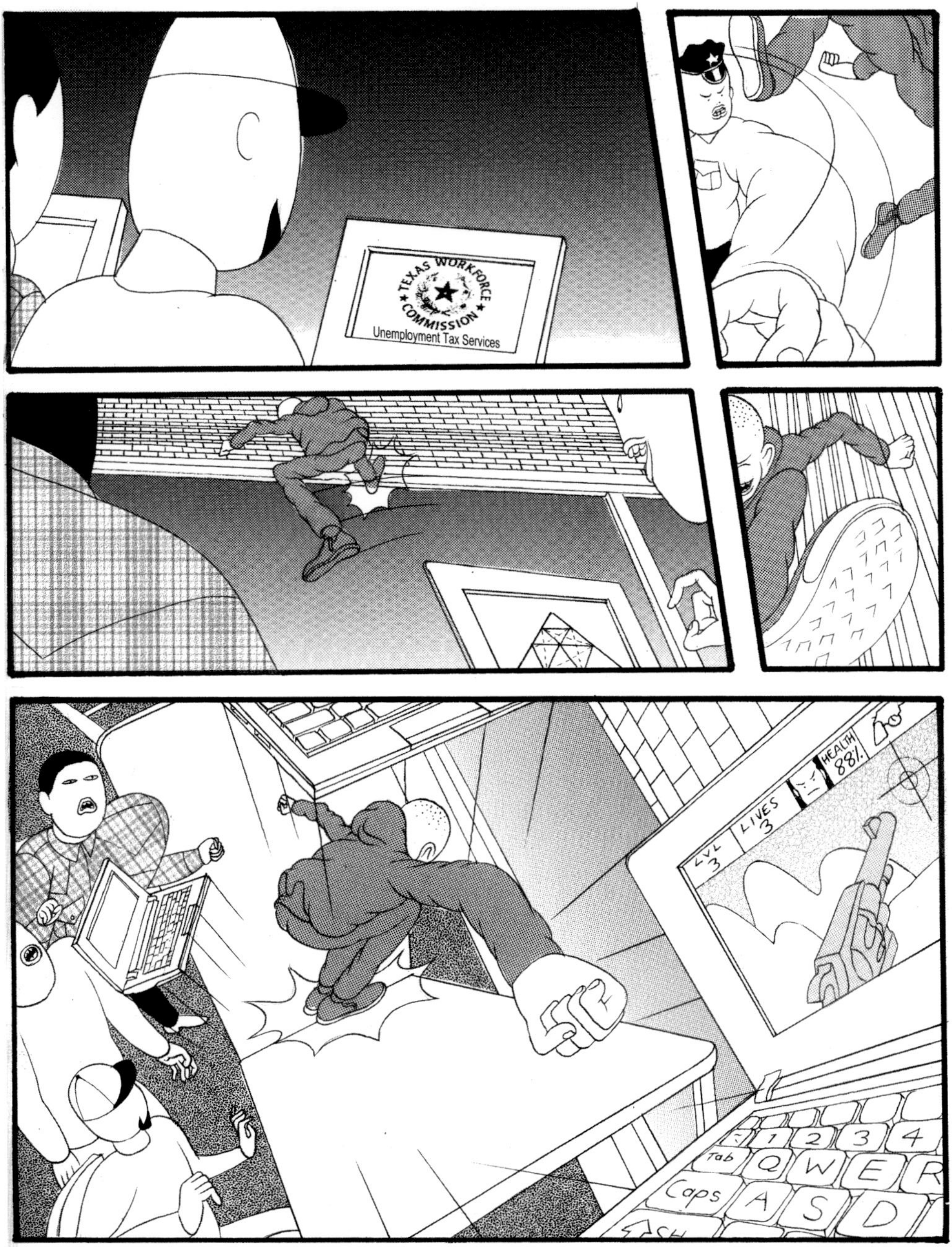
TEXAS WORKFORCE COMMISSION
Unemployment Tax Services
LVL 3
LIVES 3
HEALTH 88%
1 2 3 4
Tab Q W E R
Caps A S D

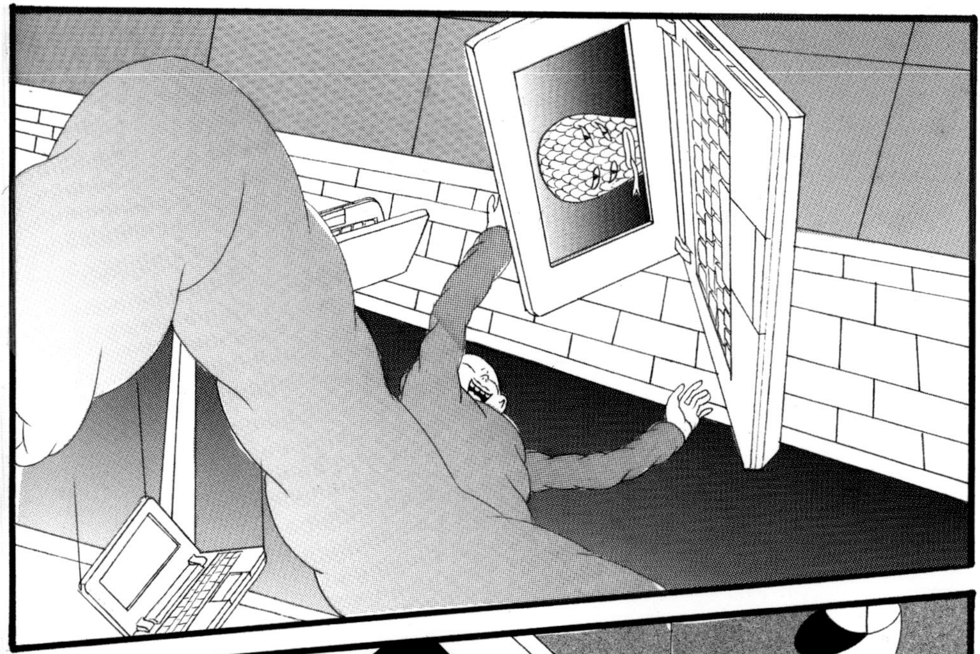

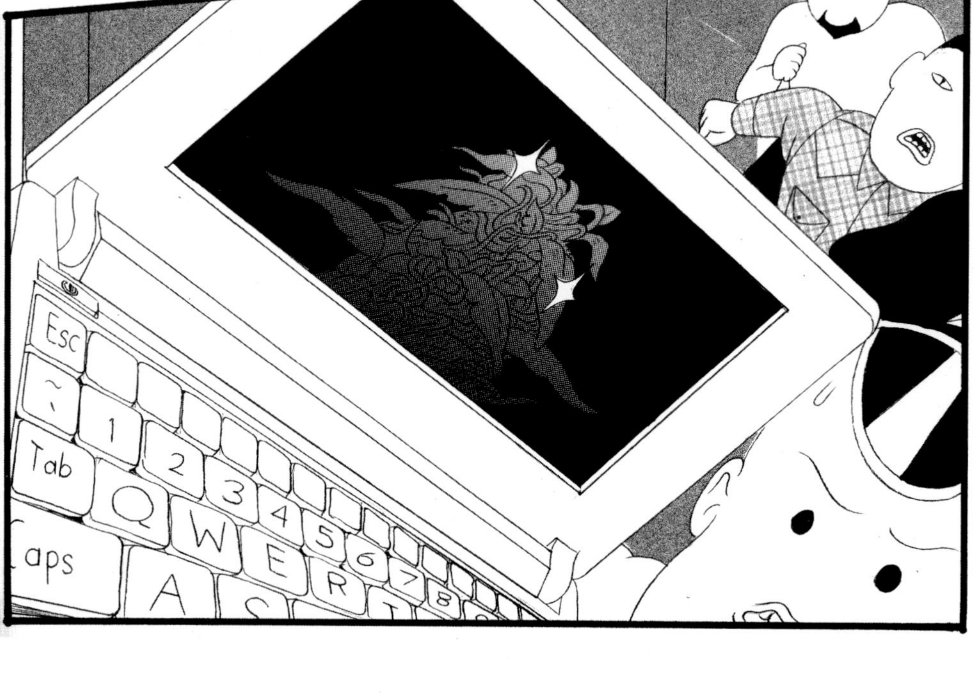
Esc
Tab
1
2
3
4
5
6
7
8
Q
W
E
R
A

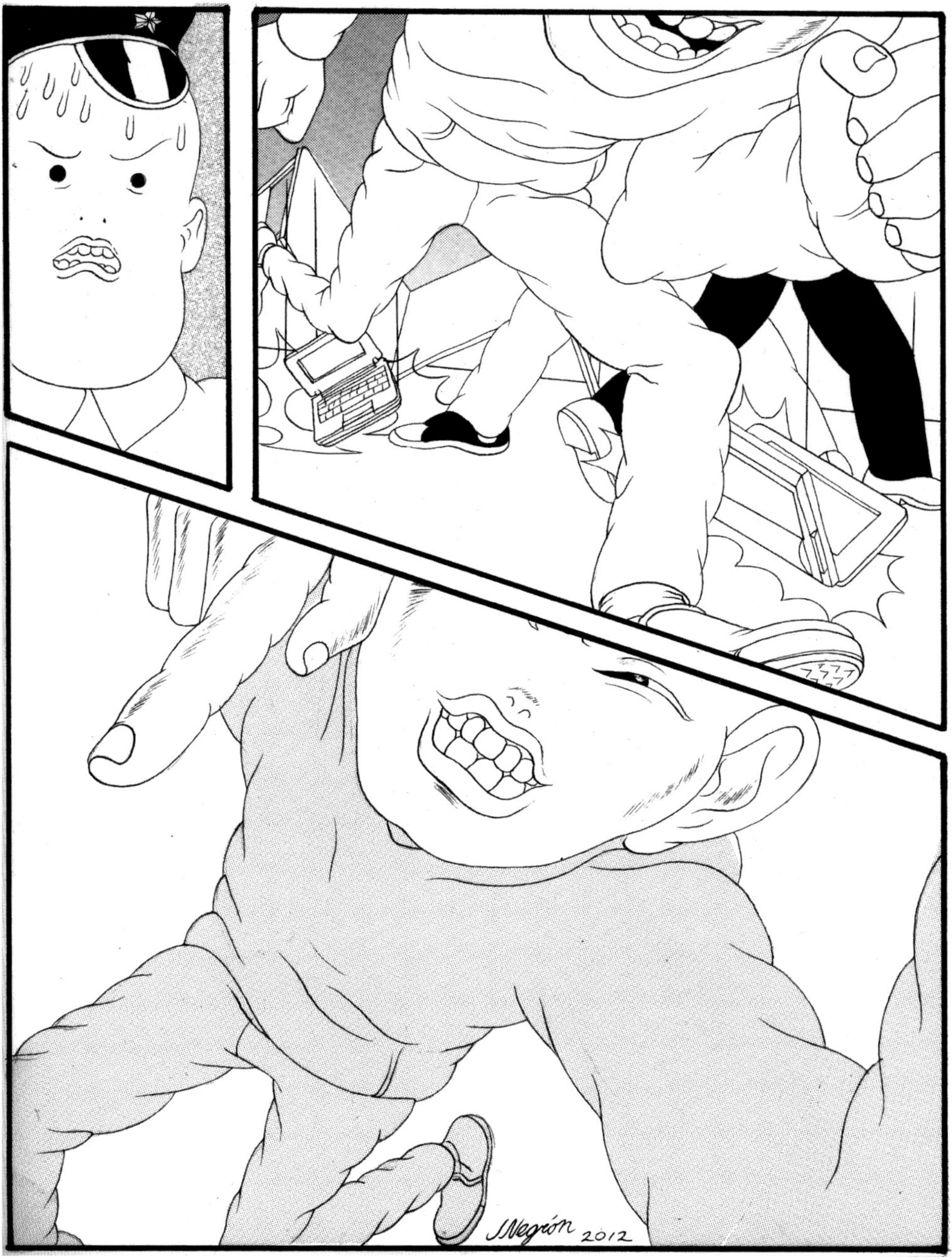
J Negrón 2012

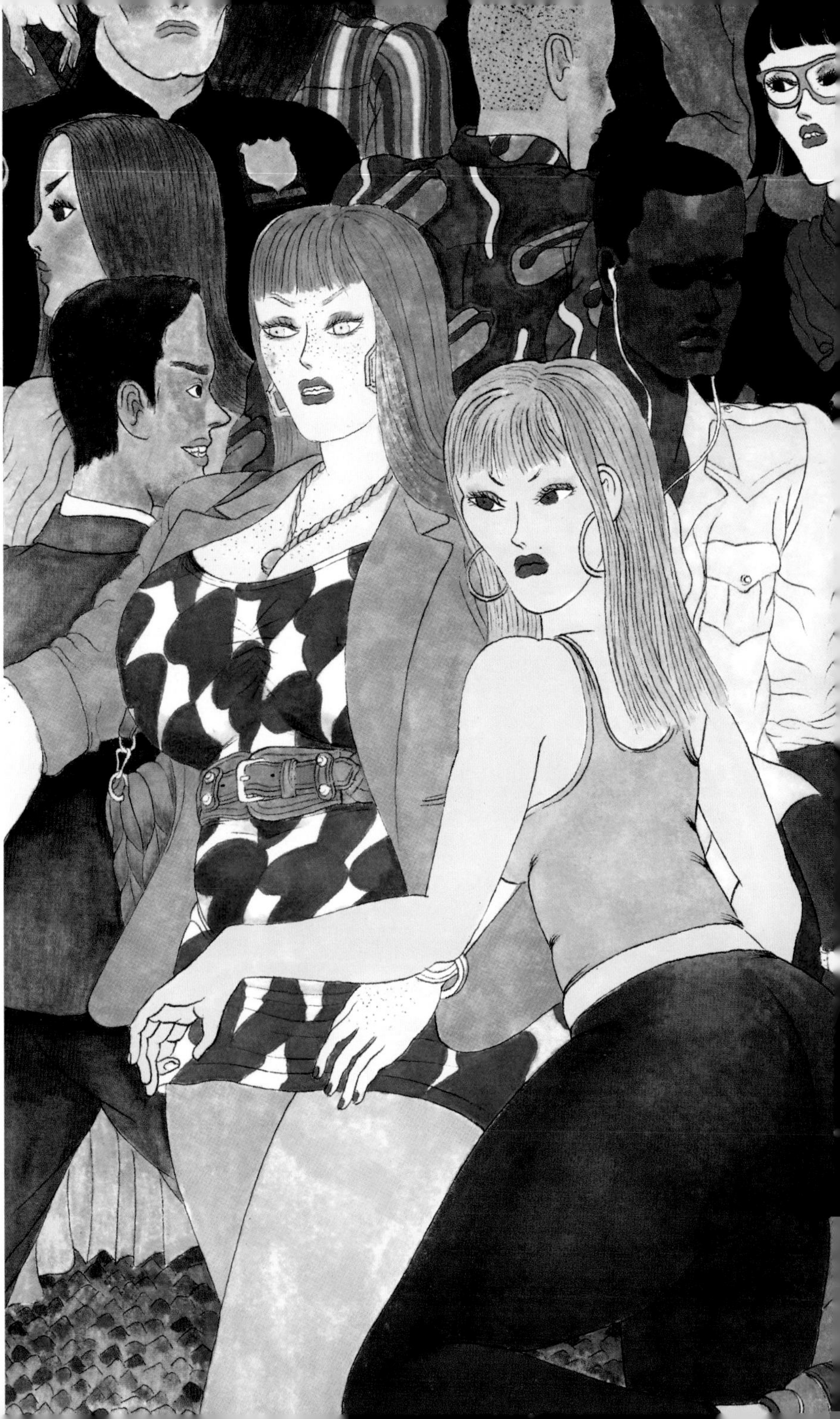

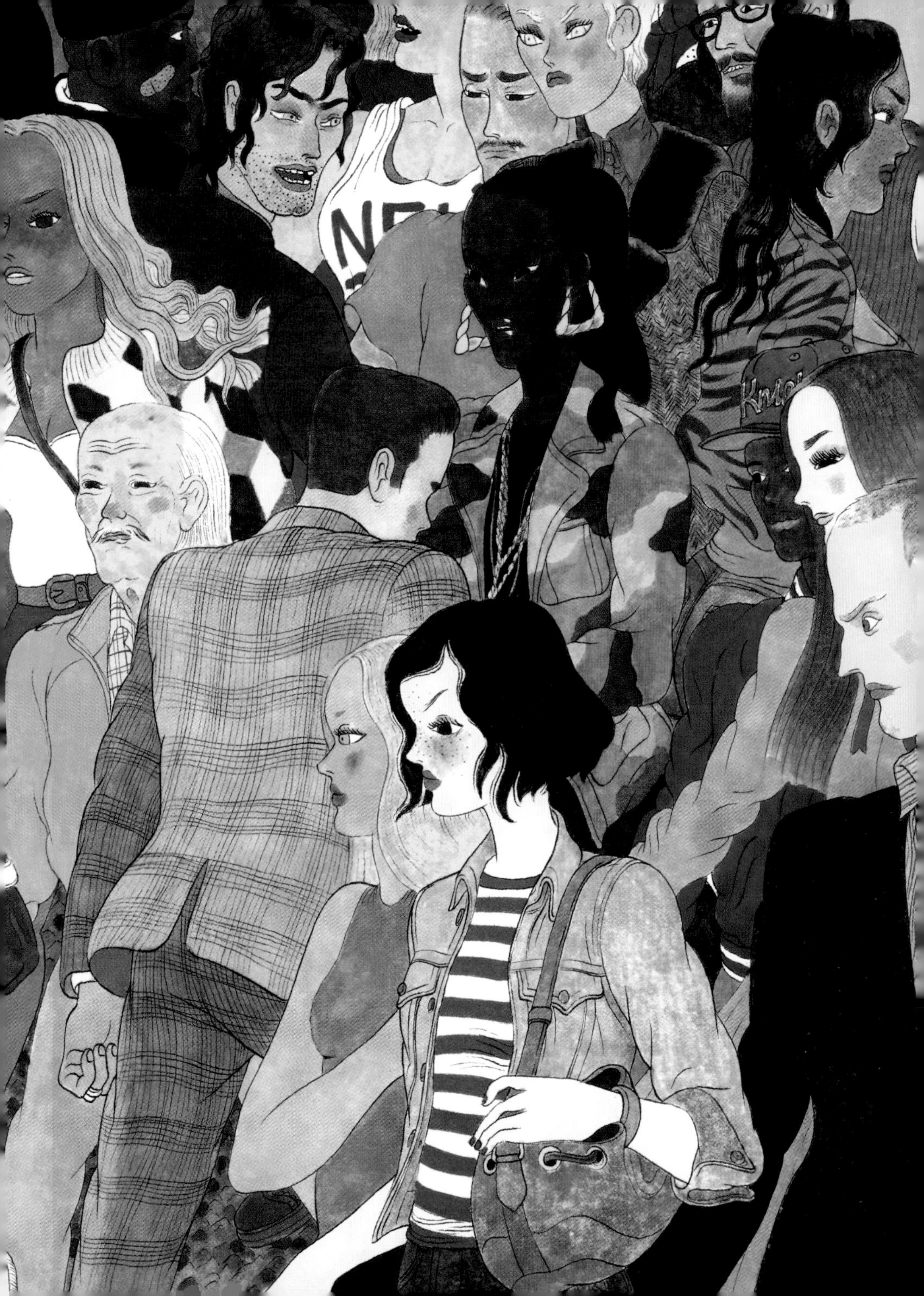

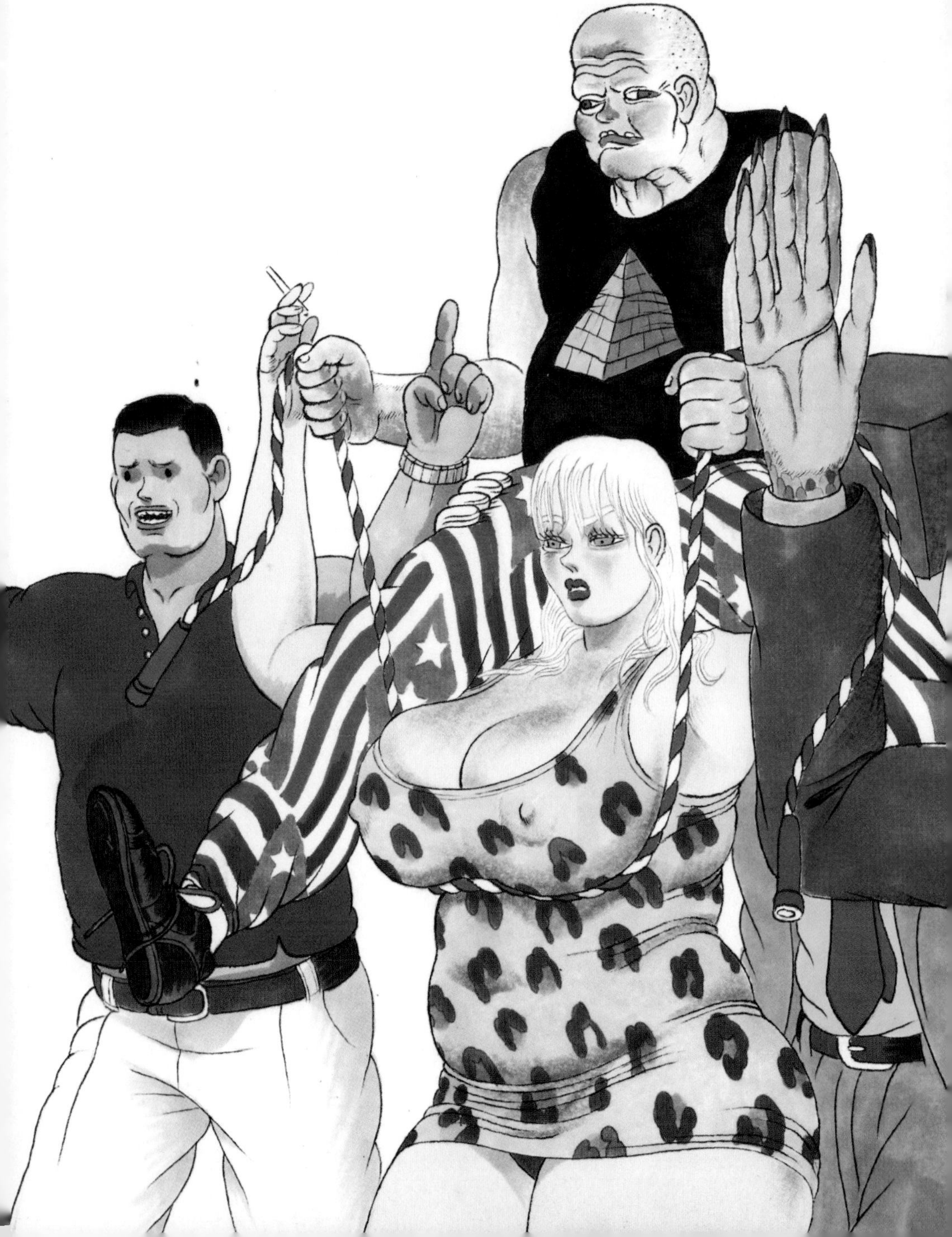

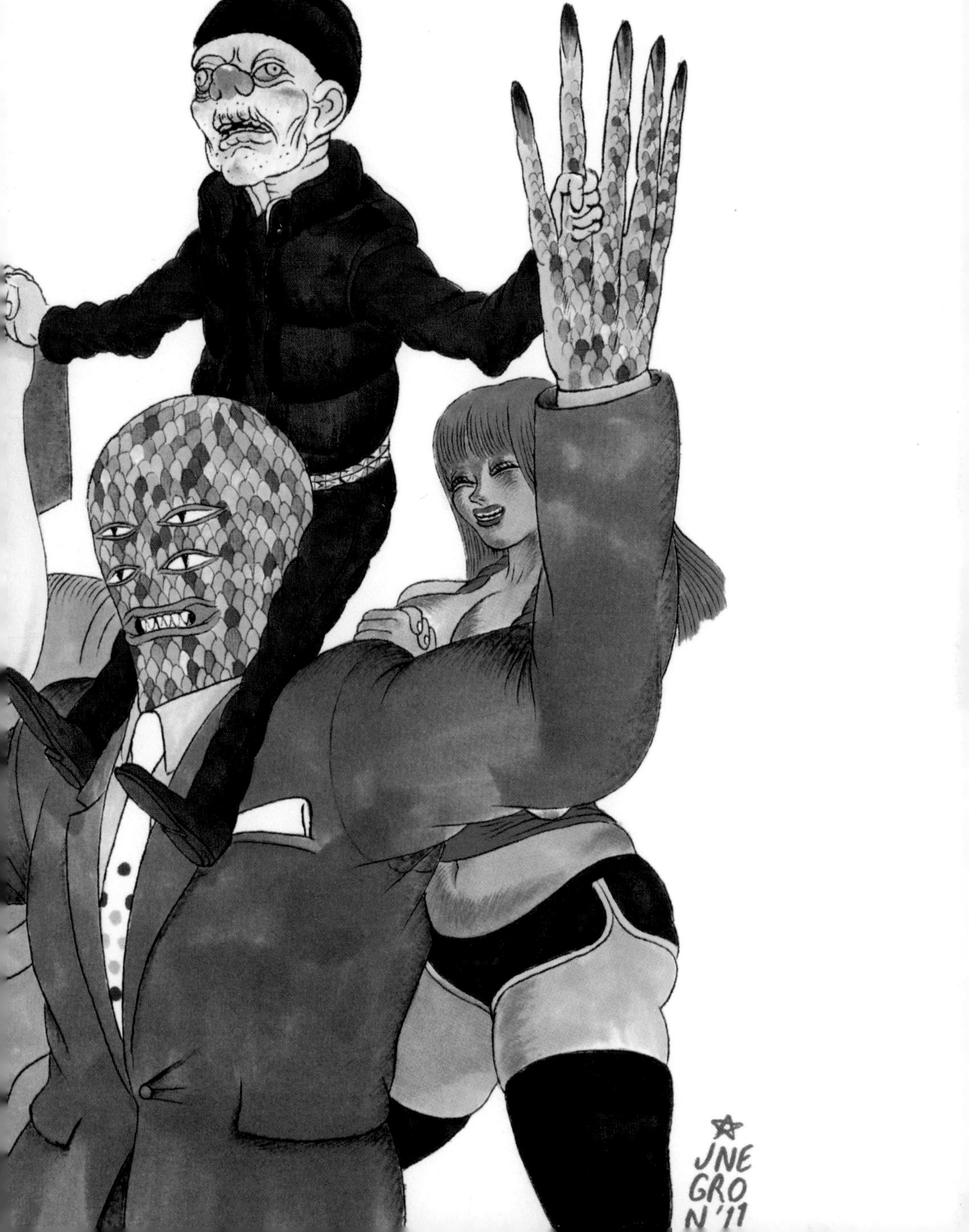
JNE
GRO
N'11

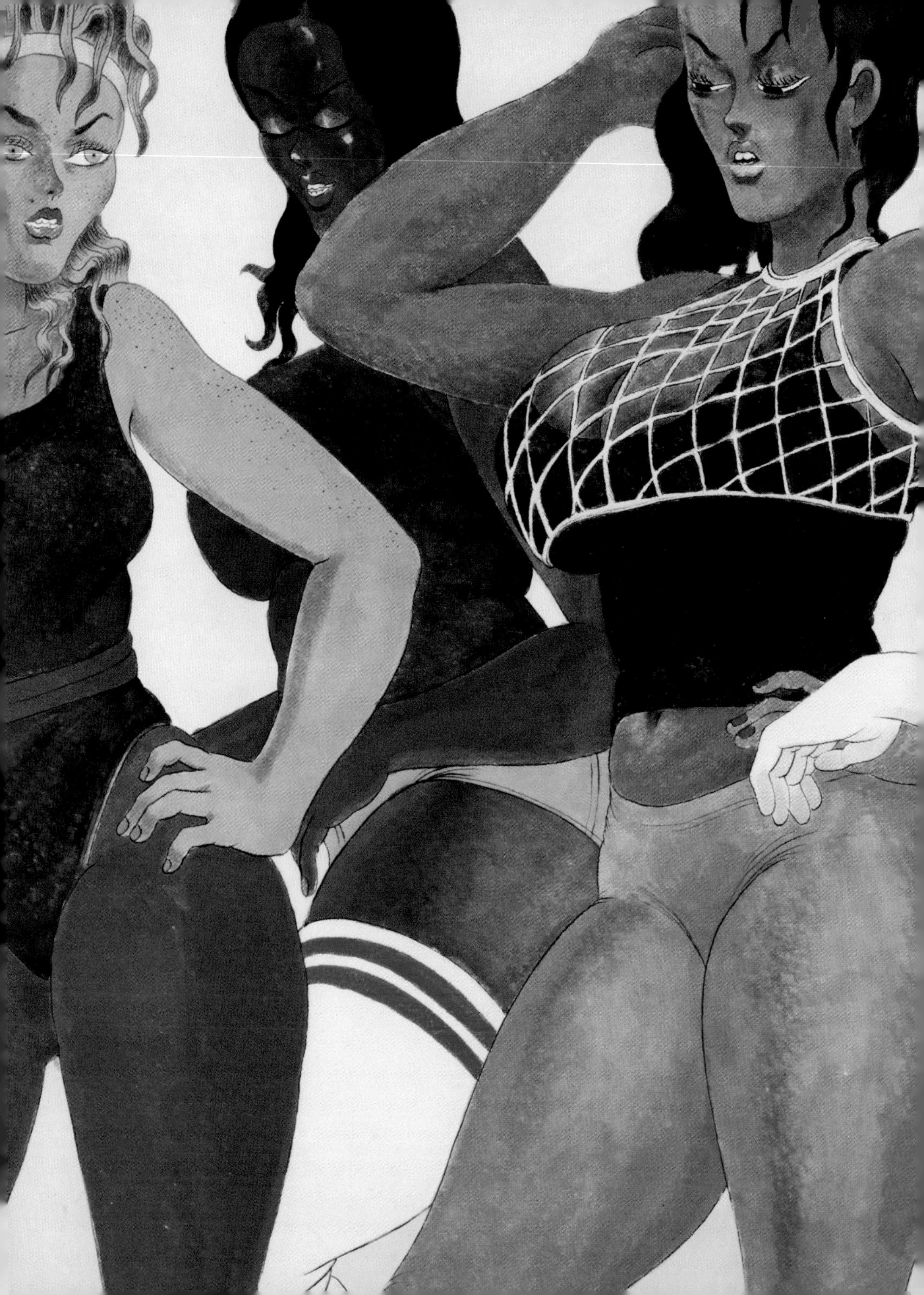

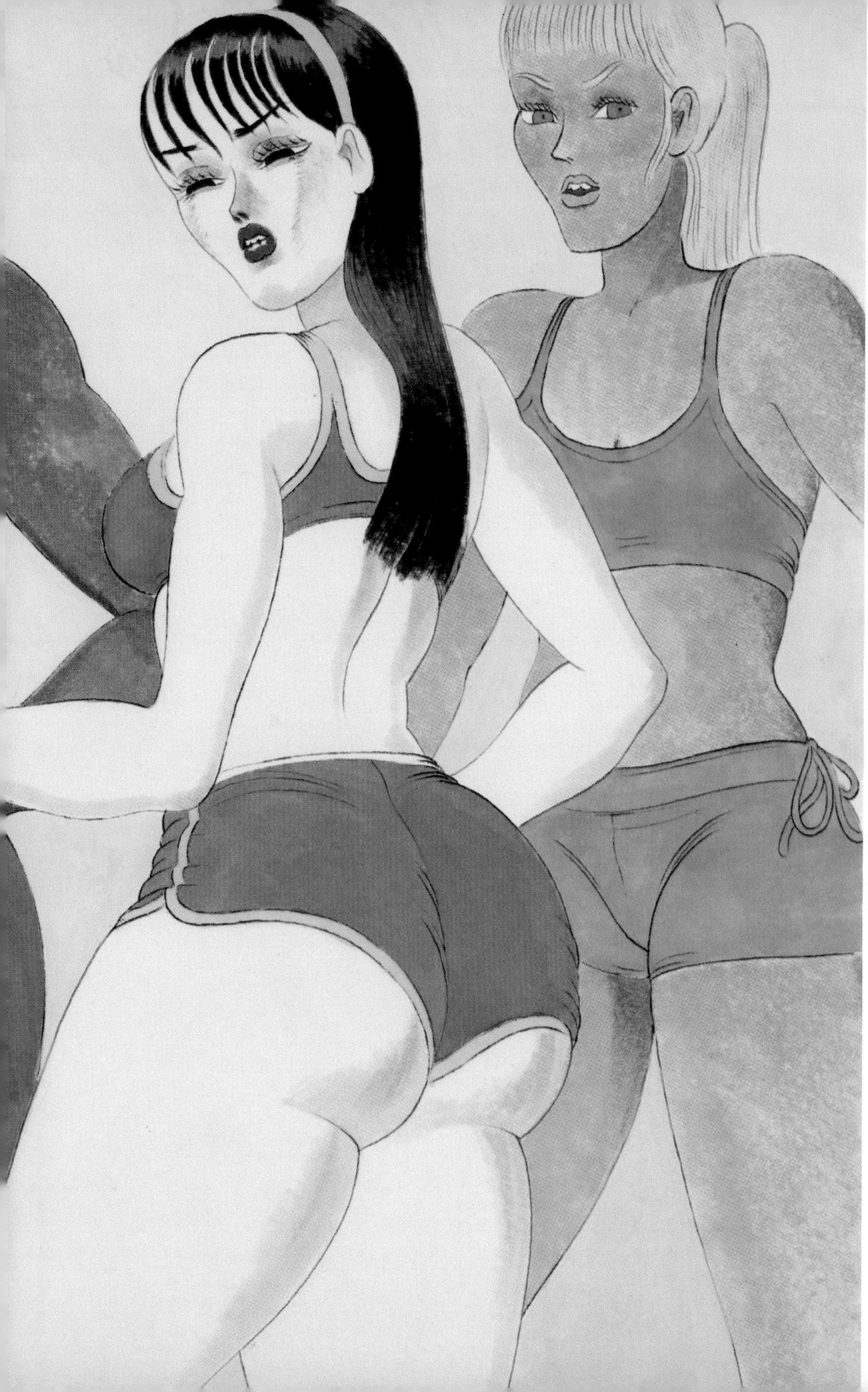

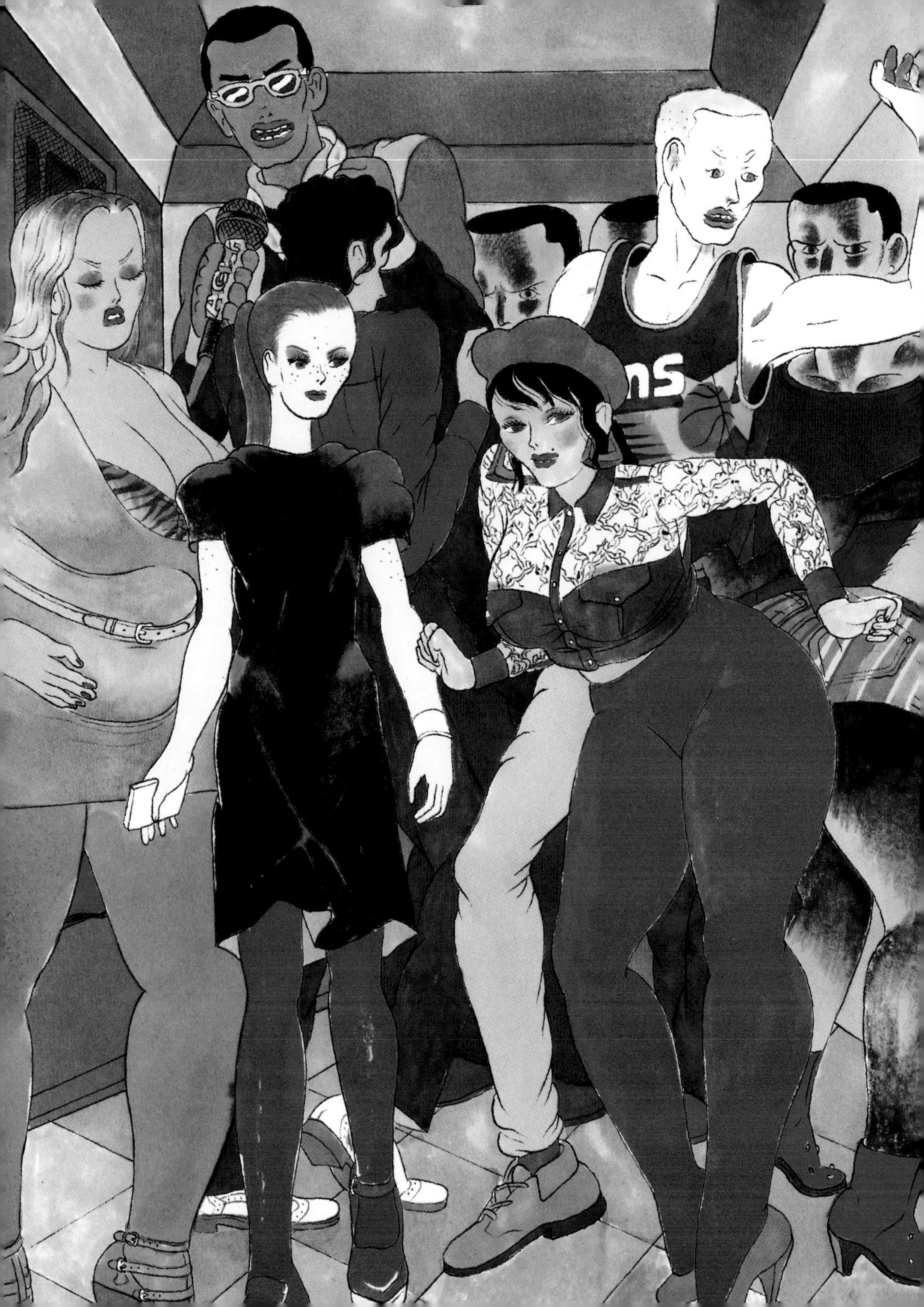

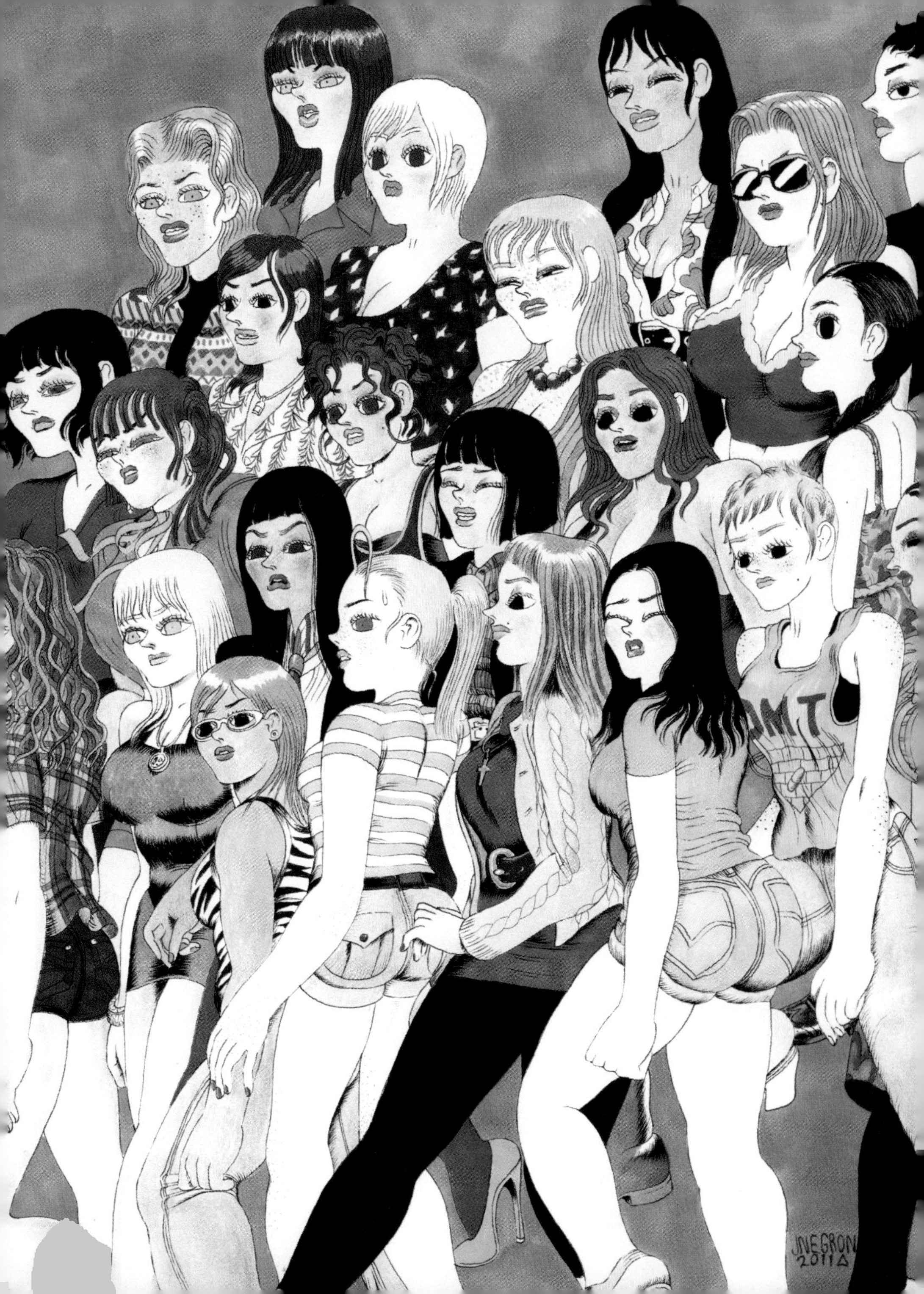
DMT
JNEGRON
2011

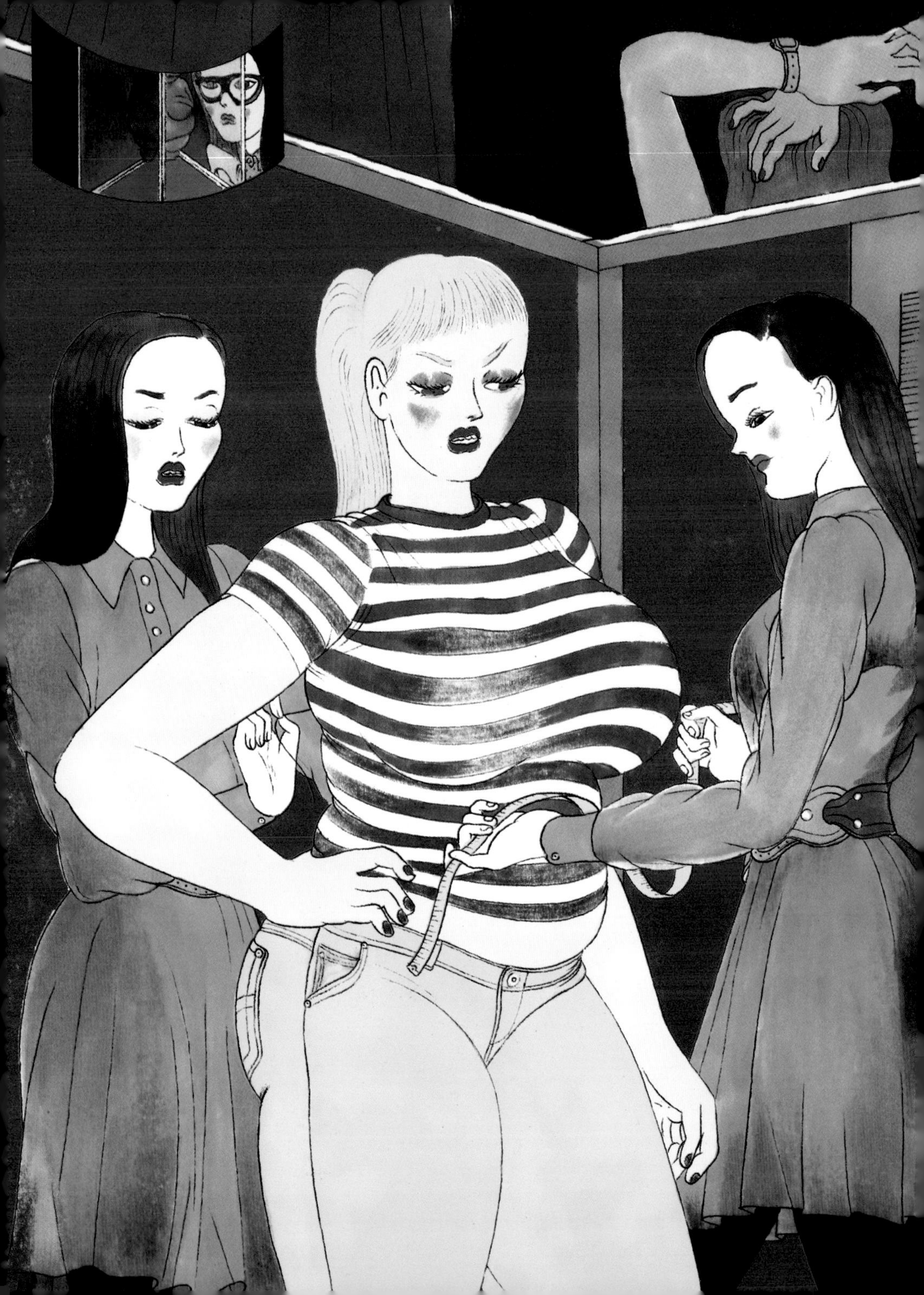

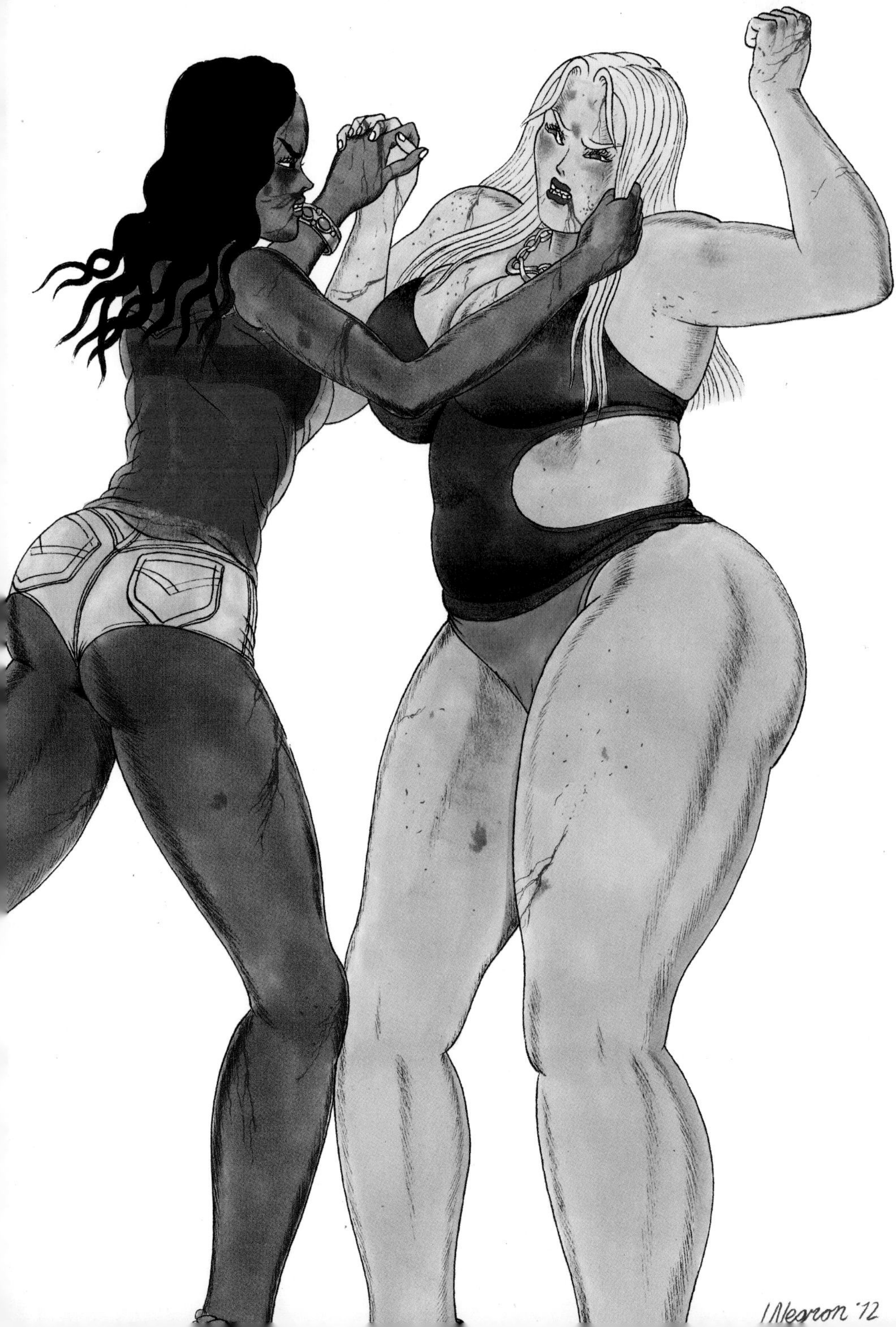

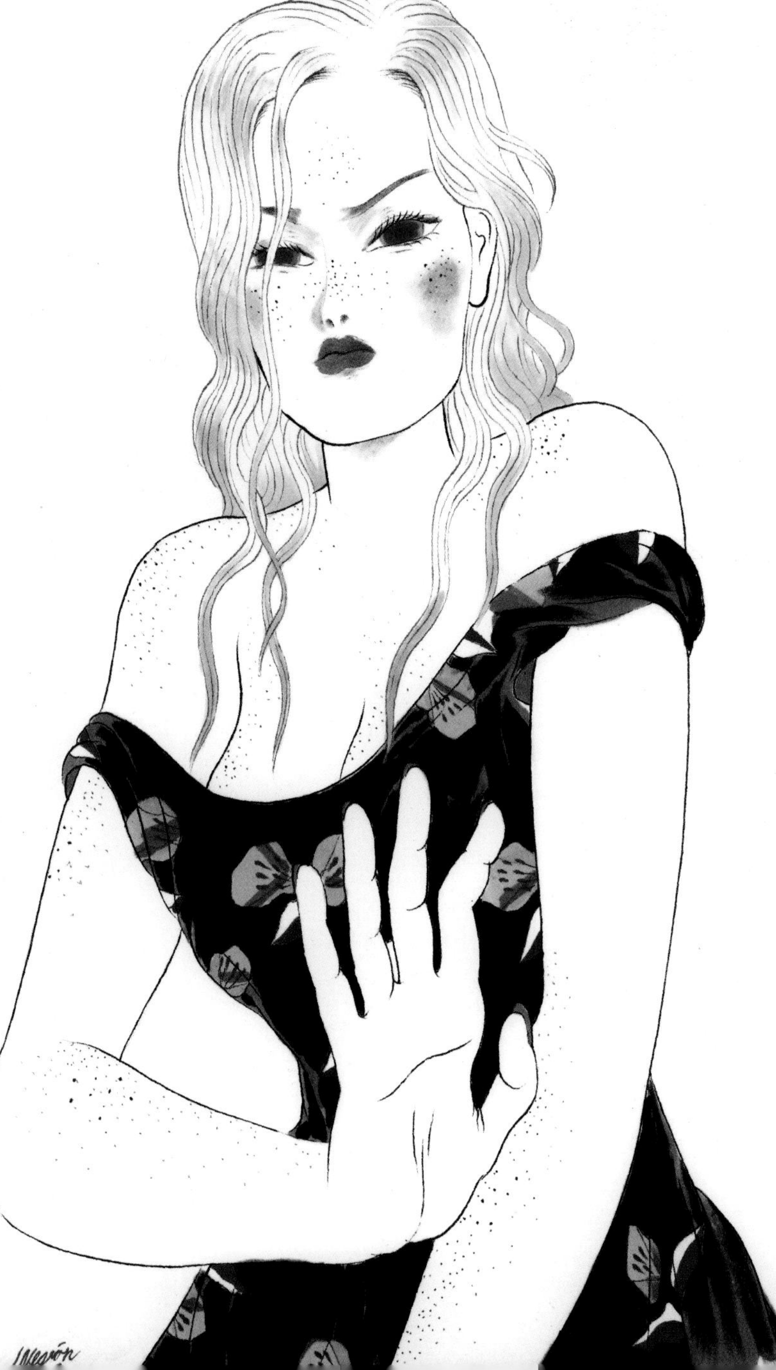

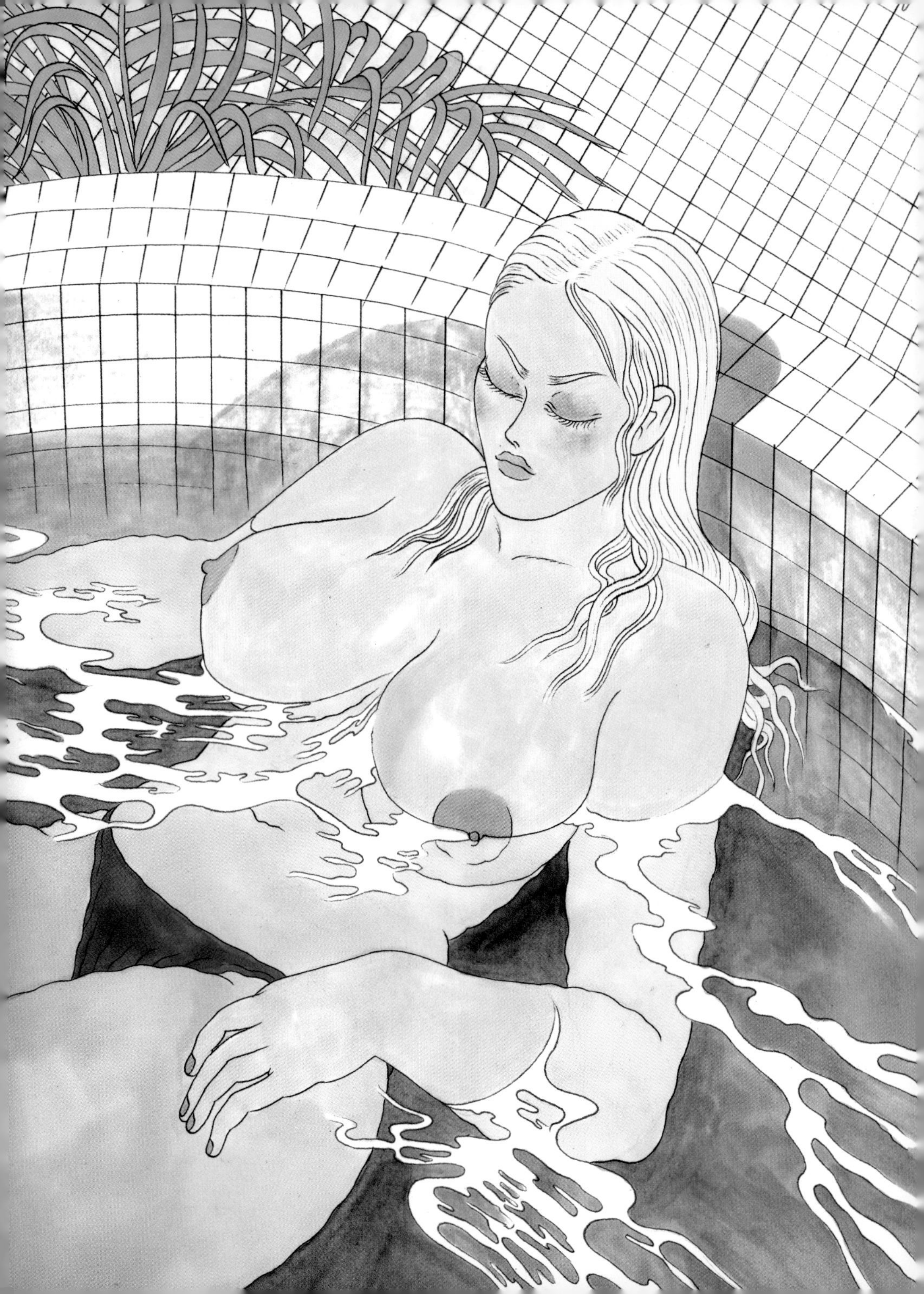

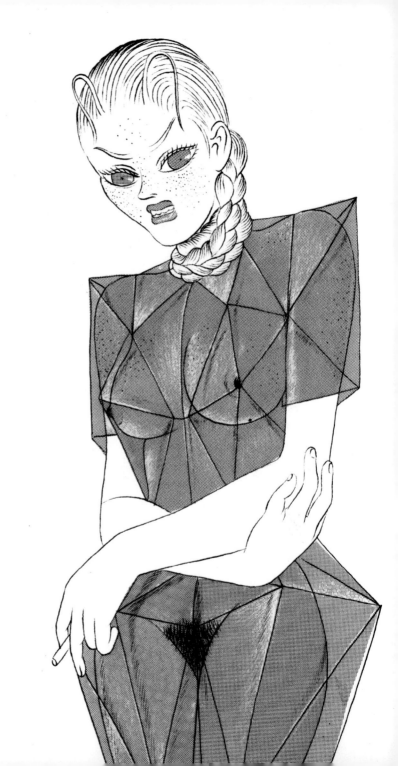

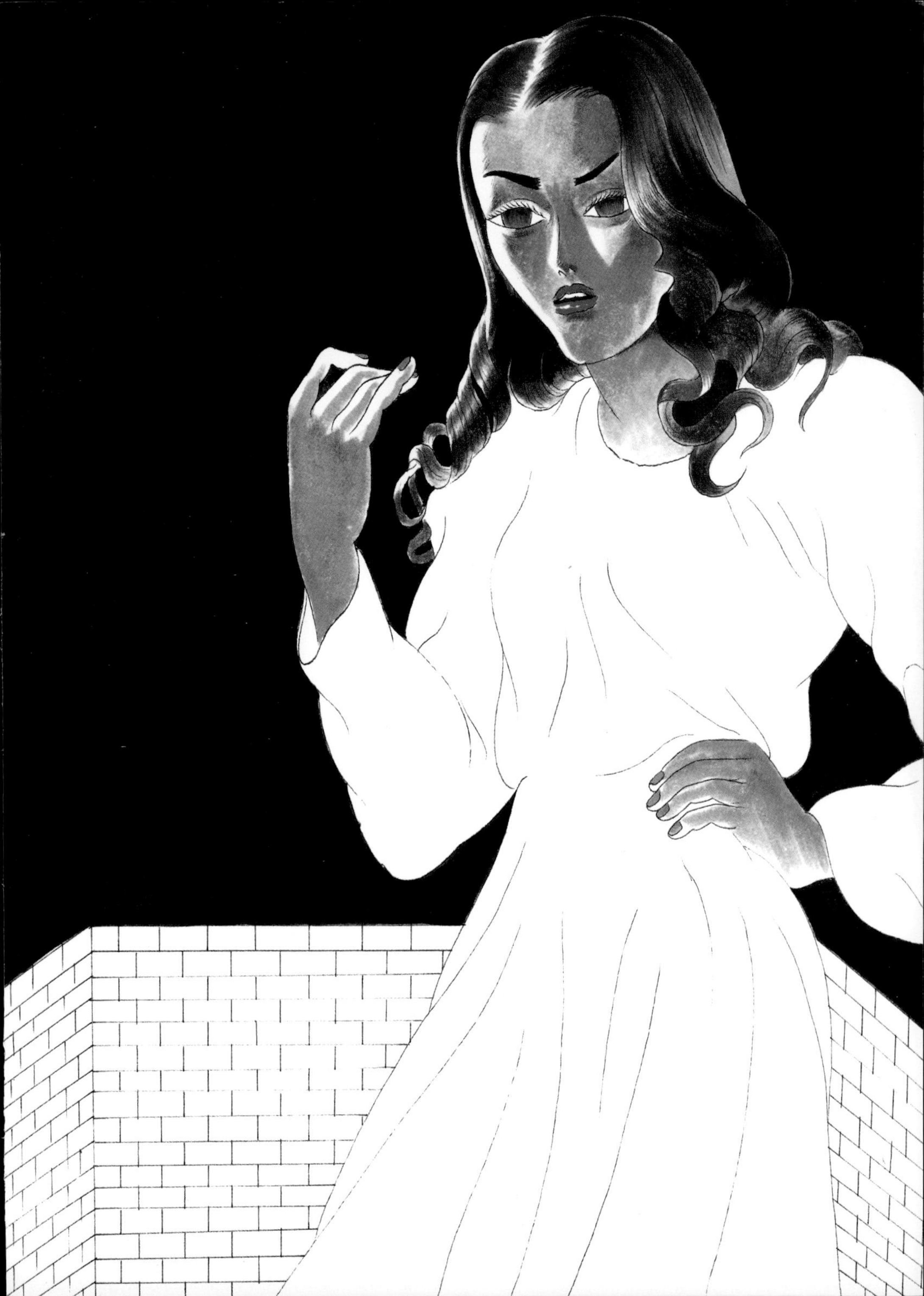

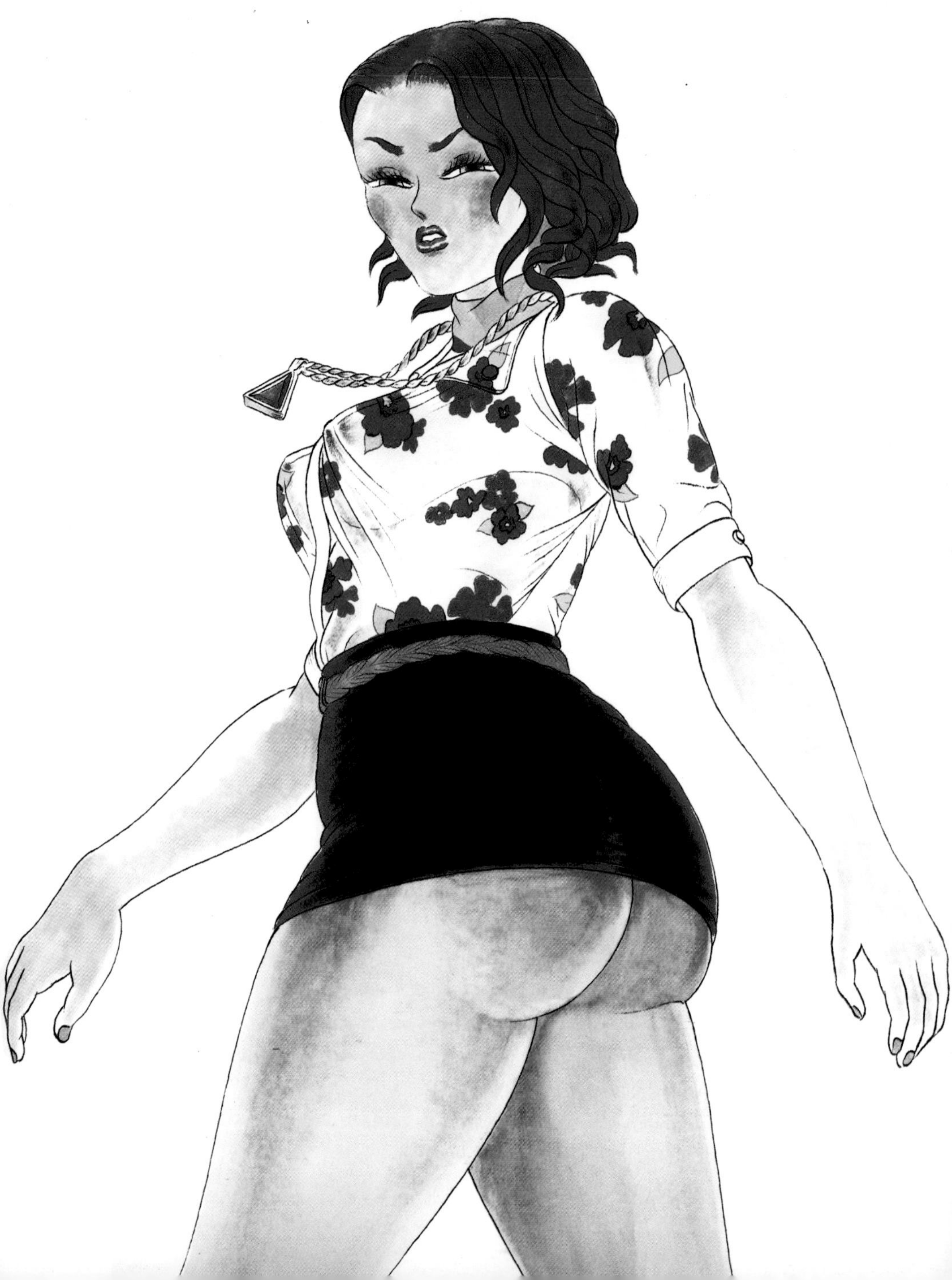

OOOH THAT'S A TASTY LOOKIN' HOTDOG

MMM I CAN'T EAT THE WHOLE THING, WANNA BITE?

MMMHMMM...

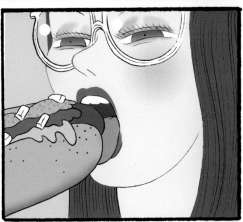
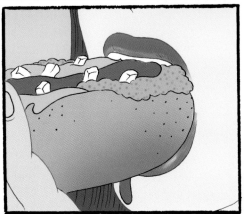

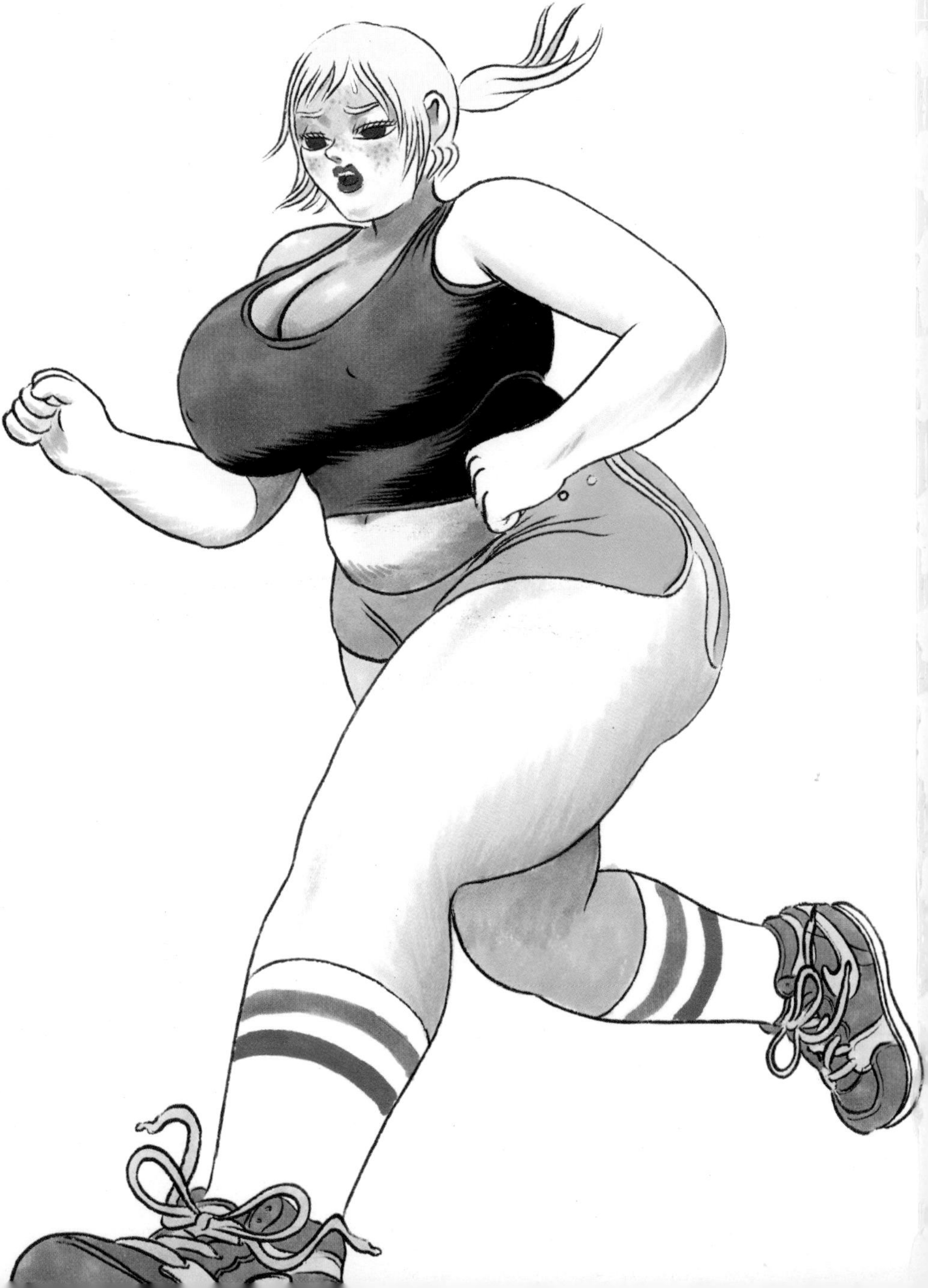